on track ...

Steven Wilson

Insurgentes-To The Bone

every album, every song

Nick Holmes

SONICBOND

sonicbondpublishing.com

Sonicbond Publishing Limited
www.sonicbondpublishing.co.uk
Email: info@sonicbondpublishing.co.uk

First Published in the United Kingdom 2026
First Published in the United States 2026

British Library Cataloguing in Publication Data:
A Catalogue record for this book is available from the British Library

ISBN 978-1-78952-317-1

Typeset in ITC Garamond Std & ITC Avant Garde Gothic
Printed and bound in England

Graphic design and typesetting: Full Moon Media

Follow us on social media:
Twitter: https://twitter.com/SonicbondP
Instagram: www.instagram.com/sonicbondpublishing_/
Facebook: www.facebook.com/SonicbondPublishing/

Linktree QR code:

Dedicated to my father, John Charles Holmes
(7 August 1933 – 20 April 1994),
under whose benign influence my
lifetime's musical journey began.

Acknowledgements

Thanks to Gill and Andrew for their good-humoured
and thoughtful proof-reading and suggestions.
And to David for his patience and kindness.

Special thanks to Steven Wilson and all the musicians
who have shared his musical vision, without whom ...

on track ...

Steven Wilson

Insurgentes-To The Bone

Contents

Introduction

Steven John Wilson was born on 3 November 1967 in Kingston-on-Thames in South West London. When he was eight, his parents moved to Hemel Hempstead in Hertfordshire and he has lived there or in London ever since. His father was an electronics engineer who made the young Wilson various pieces of electronic music equipment, on which he used to experiment. This eventually led to Wilson creating a home studio in his parents' home, which he called 'No Man's Land', where he recorded and mixed several albums to a very high sonic standard. A self-taught musician who plays guitar, bass and keyboards, as well as singing lead vocals, Wilson has also learned how to remix classic albums, to create Grammy-nominated 5.1 surround sound mixes, and more recently, to mix in immersive Dolby Atmos sound.

Wilson was in various bands at school, then formed an electronic music duo called Altamont with Simon Vocking, who lived locally. He formed a prog rock band called Karma. He also recorded electronic music under the name No Man is an Island Except the Isle of Man. He was joined by singer Tim Bowness and the band became No-Man. In 1990, the band's single 'Colours' was Single of the Week in two respected music papers, *Melody Maker* and *Sounds*. The band continued to get good press and signed publishing and record deals, allowing Wilson to give up his day job as a computer engineer. But in the meantime, Wilson was also working on another project that was eventually to become much more successful. Porcupine Tree began as a joke, a fictitious band formed with his friend Malcolm Stocks. He made up a back catalogue for the band and started recording music under the name Porcupine Tree. The release of music on cassette eventually led to the first official Porcupine Tree album, *On The Sunday Of Life*, a compilation of early material, in 1992. Initially a solo project, on later albums, Wilson was joined by Richard Barbieri (keyboards), Chris Maitland (drums, later replaced by Gavin Harrison) and Colin Edwin (bass). Wilson wrote almost all the music and lyrics for the band. Porcupine Tree toured extensively and released ten studio albums up to 2009.

In 2008, Wilson released his first solo album, *Insurgentes*, during a very busy and creative few years when he worked on: albums with Porcupine Tree (*Fear Of A Blank Planet* in 2008, and *The Incident* in 2009), his collaboration with Mikael Åkerfeldt from Swedish progressive metal band Opeth (this began in 2010 and led to the release of *Storm Corrosion* in 2012); an album with No-Man (*Schoolyard Ghosts* in 2008); a live album as Bass Communion (*Chiaroscuro* in 2009); an album with Aviv Geffen under the Blackfield name (*Blackfield II* in 2007); remixes of several King Crimson albums that were released in 2010 and 2011.

Porcupine Tree's last two albums at this point brought Wilson real chart success for the first time – *Fear Of A Blank Planet* (number 31 in the UK; number 59 in the US) and *The Incident* (number 23 in the UK; number 25 in the US). In October 2010, the band played to a packed Royal Albert Hall in

London (capacity: c. 5,000) compared with their first gig at the Nag's Head in High Wycombe, England, in 1993 (capacity: c. a few 100). Many musicians in Wilson's position would have continued working with Porcupine Tree. With a very strong back catalogue, a dedicated and growing fanbase, and a reputation for innovative and immersive live performances and virtuoso musicians, the band could have continued with great success for years. Instead, after the October 2010 gig, Wilson put the band on hiatus, and for a long time, it appeared that there would be no more music or tours (until the unexpected release of *Closure/Continuation* in June 2022 and subsequent tour).

Following his chart success with Porcupine Tree, it may have shocked Wilson that his first solo album only charted at number 116 in the UK and failed to chart in the US. But his determination to continue with his solo career was finally vindicated in chart terms when his fifth and sixth solo albums, *To The Bone* (2017) and *The Future Bites* (2021), both went top five in the UK. In August 2017, Clive Morgan of *The Telegraph* described Wilson as 'probably the most successful British musician most people have never heard of.'

Wilson has often had an uneasy relationship with fame, putting artistic integrity before commercial success, although sometimes bemoaning the fact that his obvious talent has been largely ignored. He's also refused to settle for a comfortable formula, constantly reinventing and challenging himself and his audience. Although his music has often been described as 'prog rock' – he has sometimes even been called 'The King of Prog' – he resists being categorised. And it would be difficult to describe some of the most recent solo albums – *The Future Bites, To The Bone* and *The Harmony Codex* – as purely prog. In 2025, he released *The Overview*, a space-themed album consisting of only two tracks, which marked a partial return to prog rock. The album reached number three on the album charts. Wilson toured the album extensively in 2025, with a film made by Miles Skarin of Crystal Spotlight.

The difficulty in categorising his music is perhaps part of the reason for Wilson's relative lack of commercial success as a solo artist. It's difficult to reconcile the intricate jazz-prog of 'Raider II' (*Grace For Drowning*) with the joyous pop of 'Permanating' (*To The Bone*), and the electronic disco of 'Personal Shopper' (*The Future Bites*). And the indie-band noise-rock of much of *Insurgentes* sits uncomfortably with the proggy virtuosity of *The Raven That Refused To Sing* and much of *Hand. Cannot. Erase.*

But there are threads that run through his work. A restless intelligence and a profound way of looking at the world, often expressed in a fascinating concept for an individual album. The highest possible standards of production and mixing. A gift for melody and hooks. Skilful and innovative arrangements across long-form prog epics and simple pop songs. Very high-quality musicianship, both from himself and his collaborators. Ultimately, the ability to move those listeners who are prepared to join him on a deeply satisfying journey.

Nick Holmes, Heaton Chapel, England, 30 March 2026

Cast Of Characters

Nick Beggs (born 1961)

A British bass and Chapman Stick player, Beggs' distinctive bass solo can be heard at the start of 'Too Shy' by the English pop band Kajagoogoo, a worldwide hit in 1983.

A member of Steven Wilson's band from *Grace For Drowning* to date. He also plays with his own band, The Mute Gods.

Adam Holzman (born 1958)

American keyboard player Holzman plays on albums from *The Raven That Refused To Sing* to date. He is the son of Jac Holzman, founder of Elektra Records. A jazz player, he was the music director for Miles Davis and performs with his own band, Brave New World.

Theo Travis (born 1964)

Travis plays saxophone and clarinet on *Insurgentes*, *Grace For Drowning*, *The Raven That Refused To Sing, Hand. Cannot. Erase.* and *The Harmony Codex*, and duduk on the latter album.

In 2024, Travis released *Aeolus: One Hour Duduk Meditation*, produced by Wilson, who also added soundscapes. A jazz player, Travis has led his own quartet for over 25 years. He was a member of Gong for ten years and is currently a member of Soft Machine.

Guthrie Govan (born 1971)

Govan plays guitar on *The Raven That Refused To Sing* and *Hand. Cannot. Erase.* He began playing at the age of three. He studied English at St Catherine's College, Oxford, but dropped out to play guitar. He has performed with The Aristocrats, Asia, Hans Zimmer's touring band and his own band, Erotic Cakes.

Wilson has worked with the following drummers:

Gavin Harrison (born 1963)

A member of Porcupine Tree, King Crimson and The Pineapple Thief. He has collaborated with Canadian bass player Antoine Fafard and released a solo album, *Cheating The Polygraph* – a jazzy reimagining of some of Porcupine Tree's songs – in 2005. He plays on Wilson's *Insurgentes* album.

Nic France (born 1956)

As a boy, he played piano and was a chorister at Ely Cathedral. He began playing drums at the age of 14. He was a founder member of English jazz group Loose Tubes and played with jazz band Working Week. He has toured extensively as a jazz and rock drummer. He plays on Wilson's *Insurgentes* album.

Marco Minnemann (born 1970)
German drummer Minnemann is a member of The Aristocrats (with Govan and bass player Bryan Beller), Beggs' The Mute Gods and the rock supergroup The Sea Within, and has toured with guitarist Joe Satriani. He plays on Wilson's *The Raven That Refused To Sing* and *Hand. Cannot. Erase.* albums.

Craig Blundell (born 1973)
An English drummer who began playing at the age of three. He is a prog rock drummer, teacher and drum clinician. He has played with Steve Hackett and recorded two albums with Beggs and Holzman under the name Trifecta. He plays on Wilson's *To The Bone, The Harmony Codex* and *The Overview* albums.

Other Characters

Ninet Tayeb (born 1983)
Tayeb sings vocals on *Hand. Cannot. Erase., To The Bone* and *The Harmony Codex*. A major star in her native Israel, she won the Israeli equivalent of the British TV show *Pop Idol* in 2003 and has released several solo albums.

Lasse Hoile (born 1973)
Born in Denmark, Hoile is a photographer and filmmaker who began working with Wilson on Porcupine Tree's *In Absentia* (2002). He has designed album covers, taken photographs and directed films and videos for Wilson.

Hajo Müller (born 1965)
Born in Düsseldorf, Germany, Müller is an artist (painting and drawing), photographer and designer. He first began working with Wilson on the 2009 Porcupine Tree album *The Incident*. He has designed covers and Deluxe Edition books for Wilson's albums.

Insurgentes (2008)

Personnel:
Steven Wilson: vocals, guitars, pianos, keyboards, synthesisers, harmonium, Mellotron, bass guitar, percussion, programming, ambient noise, loops, glockenspiel
Gavin Harrison: drums and cymbals
Tony Levin: bass
Mike Outram: electric guitar
Dirk Serries: guitar drones
Jordan Rudess: piano
Clodagh Simonds: vocals on 'Significant Other'
Susana Moyaho: vocals on 'Only Child'
Sand Snowman: acoustic and processed acoustic guitars, recorders
Theo Travis: wah-flute, clarinet, saxophone
Michiyo Yagi: 17-string bass koto, 21-string koto
The London Session Orchestra: strings
Recorded at 'various international locations', St Bartholomew's Church, Brighton, Red Room Recorders, Tampa Bay, Florida, Sound Pot, Tokyo, Angel Studio, London
Produced and mixed by Steven Wilson
Mastering: Andy VanDette (stereo mix); Steven Wilson (5.1 mix)
Cover and photography by Lasse Hoile
Release date: November 2008
Remastered version: March 2016
Chart placings: UK: 116, US: did not chart
Running time: 55:22
Record label: Headphone Dust, Tonefloat (limited editions)
Current edition: Kscope

Insurgentes is Steven Wilson's first solo studio album, released in November 2008. It could be argued that it isn't his first solo album at all, as early Porcupine Tree albums were essentially solo projects – he wrote, performed and produced all the music, although many of the lyrics were written by his schoolfriend Alan Duffy. In an interview with the German *Recording Magazin*, on YouTube in January 2014, he said: 'The reason I didn't make this music with Porcupine Tree is that it's not Porcupine Tree music.' There's a sense of relief that he was able to express his own musical personality fully for the first time since Porcupine Tree had become a full band. Although he continued to write all the music and all the lyrics for the band, even when it became a four-piece, he felt that he had to match the songwriting to the musical sensibilities of the other band members.

Wilson told Stephen Bennett of *Tape Op Magazine* in September 2009: 'I don't have a fantastically articulate answer as to why this is a 'Steven Wilson' record – it just felt right.' He had been releasing solo records as the Bass

Communion project since the 1990s and released another album, *Cenotaph,* under that name three years later. Perhaps the difference is that the Bass Communion project is ambient music that he described on his website as 'experiments in texture', whereas music released under his own name is usually written for him to tour with a full band.

In March 2009, Wilson told Stephen Humphries of *PopMatters*: 'Unlike many musicians who are quite content to mine one particular seam in style terms, I've never been happy to do that.' On *Insurgentes,* he explores prog rock, ambient music, industrial noise music, melodic songs, art rock and orchestral music. Perhaps to the surprise of some Porcupine Tree fans, the one major style that is missing from the solo albums is heavy metal, a major part of the texture of later Porcupine Tree albums such as *In Absentia* (2002), *Fear Of A Blank Planet* (2007) and *The Incident* (2009).

If anything, the musical spirit of the album is rooted in the post-punk English bands of the 1980s. At a Twitter Listening Party in June 2020, hosted by Tim Burgess of The Charlatans, he said: 'I started exploring my influences from new wave, post-punk music, and labels like [4AD] ... Stuff like Cocteau Twins, Wire, Joy Division and The Cure.' What united these bands and provides the musical spine that runs through *Insurgentes* is an introspective quality, a glimpse of the depths of the soul, sometimes quiet, sometimes turbulent. In March 2009, Wilson told 'Deadwing' of *MetalUnderground*: 'It's a very eclectic record, and I think it does hang together and it is a cohesive piece. I don't think it would have been even if I made it five years ago.'

A major part of the new musical aesthetic is the introduction of extreme noise music. As Wilson told Bennett, 'I'm obviously aspiring to make records that sound very good, but within these, you can have very lo-fi sounds.' More succinctly, at one point on the Twitter Listening Party, he exclaimed with evident delight: 'NOIZE!!! I love it.' He had been listening to the noise project Merzbow, started in 1979 by the Japanese artist Masami Akita. The No-Man album *Schoolyard Ghosts,* released by Wilson and Tim Bowness in May 2008, includes 'Pigeon Drummer', which combines haunting melodic passages with sudden Nine Inch Nails-style white noise, to compelling effect. He uses the same technique on several tracks on *Insurgentes.* He probably couldn't have done this with Porcupine Tree. As he told Humphries, 'Noise is very much an acquired taste.'

Some critics were unhappy with his new approach. In December 2008, *Dutch Progressive Rock Page (DPRP)* published a fascinating and typically perceptive round table review of the album. Ed Sanders said, 'The dreaminess and ambience of No-Man is present in some songs but is often rudely disturbed by aggressive noise instrumentation.' Perhaps Sanders was reacting to a technical rather than a musical issue; some sections of the original album release had been mastered to such a high level that there was audible distortion. This may have been part of the trend at the time to make tracks sound as loud as possible, a phenomenon that became known as the 'loudness wars.' Metallica's *Death Magnetic*, released in the same year as *Insurgentes,* was so heavily compressed that the drums sounded distorted, and thousands of fans called for it to be remastered. That's an extreme example, and the problems with the original version of *Insurgentes* are much more subtle. Nevertheless, it was remastered and rereleased only eight years later, most unusual for a modern, well-recorded album. Analysis of the waveforms of the remastered version shows that the distortion on the loudest parts of the music has disappeared. The distortion that remains is part of the music, so it seems that Sanders had picked up on something.

The title *Insurgentes*, meaning 'insurgents' or 'rebels', appealed to Wilson because, as he told Bennett, 'It seemed like a perfect title as I've been going against what the music industry expects and what you are supposed to do to be a successful professional musician.' He took the word from the avenue that runs from North to South in Mexico City, Avenida de los Insurgentes. Parts of the album (and the supporting DVD 'road movie' documentary) were recorded in Mexico City, and Wilson saw the Insurgentes street sign many times while he was there.

The album was recorded in various countries across the world, unlike most of Wilson's records, which have largely been recorded in his home studio and in studios in London. In an interview with Dwayne Bunney of Edge Radio (Tasmania) in March 2009, Wilson recalled that he had recorded not just in Mexico City but also in Israel, Scandinavia, Japan and America as part of what he called a 'road trip experience.' But his aim was not to make what has been called 'world music', or what he described to Bennett as 'creating a kind of geographical musical encyclopaedia.' Instead, he enjoyed travelling the world, meeting other musicians and discovering 'how these wonderful musicians could enhance and contribute to my existing vision.'

Given Wilson's very strong background as a writer of concept albums for Porcupine Tree, does his first true 'solo' album have a unifying lyrical concept? The surprising answer is that he recorded it in a completely different way, improvising the lyrics, as he said on the Twitter Listening Party, 'just for the sound of them.' He told Jeff at *MetalStorm* in April 2009 that normally he spent a lot of time agonising over lyrics, trying to give them 'deep meanings and very strong senses.' For *Insurgentes,* he felt they were less important and were part of the music, because the lyrics were improvised, 'somehow they're more natural and maybe have more emotion and feeling.' This meant that 'maybe some logical sides of the lyrics are missing'. He told Humphries, 'There are meanings there, but I'm probably as unsure about the meanings as anyone.'

Wilson had previously experimented with improvised lyrics on 'Flicker' from the Porcupine Tree album *The Incident* (2009). On that track, the lyrics feel rather unfinished, an unfiltered stream of consciousness. Wilson told Frank Jenks of the *Listen In FULL* podcast in August 2010 that, paradoxically, he wanted the *Insurgentes* lyrics to have meaning from an intellectual point of view. Context is everything – he mentions *The Fountain,* by the Surrealist artist Marcel Duchamp. This 1917 work – also known as *The Urinal* – is a standard porcelain urinal. By signing it and exhibiting it in an art gallery, Duchamp argued that it became a work of art, and in May 2002, a copy (the original had been lost) sold at auction for $1,185,000. Wilson told Franks that art can recontextualise found objects, and that pop music can do the same. In the case of songwriting, the context is the musical structure and instrumental timbre of the song, not to mention the fact that the lyrics usually need to be shaped to fit the song's rhythms.

Wilson told Humphries that although he had some degree of artistic control over the lyrics, they appeared out of a kind of 'dream logic', perhaps direct from his subconscious. He developed this theory in more detail in the interview with Jenks: 'What we dream has no bearing on reality ... we make leaps of logic and intellect that you would never make in a waking state.'

There's no reliable online source for the *Insurgentes* lyrics. Wilson would probably be happy about the ambiguity this creates. For instance, some online commentators suggest that the second line of the song 'Abandoner' is 'a *play* in the dark'; others suggest 'a *plague* in the dark'. (Analyses of the songs below may therefore be based on incorrect assumptions).

Insurgentes was the first time Wilson created a deluxe edition of an album. This was a financial risk – the lavish artwork in book format and additional discs are expensive to produce. As he said on Twitter, 'At the time, no-one else was doing them.' He told Bunney that the Deluxe Edition sold out – all 4,000 copies. He could've had more copies made, but it was 'a shot in the dark' as to how many to manufacture. He found it 'upsetting' that they were quickly being sold for inflated prices, as they had become collectable items, but at the time of release, 'everyone had a chance to get one.' He also said such editions are the chance for 'everyone to cherish a beautiful piece of art.' He has continued to release his solo albums in this format, and also re-released Porcupine Tree's 2002 album *In Absentia* in a deluxe edition in 2020.

On Twitter, Wilson said that *Insurgentes* is the least like prog rock of all his solo albums (although the same could also be said of parts of *To The Bone* and most of *The Future Bites*): 'In a way, it's also unique in my catalogue, as I moved towards a more traditional progressive rock sound with my next few albums.'

'Harmony Korine' (5:08)

Wilson said on Twitter he couldn't think of a name for the opening track of the album, so he randomly named it after the American film director Harmony Korine: 'I thought his name was beautiful (in contrast to his movies!).' Wilson told Stephen Humphries that Korine appealed to him as someone who works in surrealist cinema, and that 'there's a lot of surrealism on the record.' The fact that the title bears no relation to the song is 'a very surrealist approach.'

Wilson said this song was inspired by the 'shoegazer' sound of bands like Slow Dive, Kitchens of Distinction and My Bloody Valentine, indie rock bands who featured heavily distorted guitars where texture was often more important than melody or chords, and vocals were buried deep in the mix. In the *Insurgentes* video documentary, Wilson says that he began as a literal shoe gazer, staring at his feet when he played live, as he was too shy and nervous to look at the audience.

The start of the song perfectly sets up the contemplative, inward style of much of the album, leading to an epic chorus, which perhaps explains why this is one of Wilson's most popular solo songs. The opening words – 'rain come down, and fall forever' – immediately create a dystopian landscape, perhaps referencing the short story by the American science fiction writer Ray Bradbury, *The Day It Rained Forever* (1964). The dystopian feel is strengthened by the reference to draining the dirt into the wasteland, which could relate to T.S. Eliot's 1922 poem *The Waste Land*. That work uses several images of rain, most memorably perhaps at the very beginning, when the Spring rain stirs the lilac roots unwillingly to life in the dead land, describing the pain of birth. The stark picture Wilson creates is intensified by the idea of praying for sound 'to quiet the howling', suggesting a psychological dystopia, a prayer for some external noise to drown out the inner maelstrom. The sense of a terrible future is increased by the image in the second verse of crawling towards perdition.

But the chorus may bring hope; rain falling forever is replaced by the thought that action should be taken in this life, that the addressee of the song shouldn't wait forever or feel any shame in acting now. The line 'feel, afraid, to wait forever' is ambiguous, as it could also be read as meaning that the addressee will always be afraid to act, but the optimistic tone of the music in the chorus suggests that the first interpretation is more likely.

The song opens with a simple but intense indie guitar line, soon accompanied by the loose-limbed and languid drumming of Gavin Harrison of Porcupine Tree. The vocals are heavily compressed – a favourite mixing technique of Wilson's – creating a brooding atmosphere. The chorus explodes into life, the sound spreads wide across the stereo picture as if the aspect ratio has changed from 4:3 to widescreen, emphasising the contrast between the introspective verses and the anthemic chorus. The vocals remain compressed, but the soaring falsetto voice, almost drowned by an ensemble of distorted guitars, is uplifting.

The final chorus ends with a bloom of distorted guitar. In an interview with Ray McClelland of *guitarguitar.co.uk* in April 2021, Wilson described the distinctive guitar sound as a technique used by Neil Young on songs like 'Cortez The Killer' (*Zuma*, 1975) or 'Like A Hurricane' (*American Stars 'N Bars,* 1977): 'You're hearing him putting his guitar into a reverb and then into an amp with a lot of gain on it. And so, you get this sense that the reverb is always trying to break through ... Then you stop playing and get this big cloud of distorted, ugly reverb. But it's so rock 'n' roll! I love it!'

The video, mostly shot in black and white, was directed by Wilson's long-term visual collaborator Lasse Hoile. It's full of surreal dark humour, with humans wearing either birds' heads or gas masks – as Wilson himself does on the album's cover, showing his unwillingness to reveal his face or his eyes on much of his album artwork.

'Abandoner' (4:48)

On Twitter, Wilson said, 'The chord progression ... is really unusual, and the trick was finding the melody to go with it.' The basic chord sequence *is* unconventional, going from E minor to G minor, C# minor to A minor, but Wilson was still able to create a convincing melody.

The track opens with a lo-fi drum machine and the nostalgic crackle of a vinyl record. The vocals, in contrast to the previous track, are recorded very naturally without any effects, giving an intimate, tender feel. There's a strong feeling of melancholy, perhaps referring to the suicide of the addressee of the song, 'the rope you used to tie yourself', although the meaning of the song remains obscure. It's more about creating an atmosphere, something at which this song excels.

The song ends with a remarkable instrumental section, beginning with pulsing, mechanical percussion, surrounded by atmospheric chords. It then plunges into one of the darkest, most evocative instrumental passages Wilson has ever written. It's based on a very simple chromatic sequence of notes, but with very imaginative production, it's turned into a profoundly poetic sequence, somehow probing the depths of the soul. In the *Insurgentes* documentary, Wilson can be seen playing the notes on piano and guitar at No Man's Land, his home studio. On Twitter, he said, 'The claustrophobic ending section was made with the very lowest notes on a piano combined with layered baritone guitars. It's heavy like Sunn O))) or something.' As in the previous song, the sound suddenly blossoms as the stereo picture widens to create a mesmerising effect before the picture narrows and the percussive theme returns for the last 20 seconds.

The English guitar player Sand Snowman is credited with playing 'Acoustic Guitar (normal and processed)'. In March 2009, Steven Wilson told 'Deadwing' that he had recently discovered Snowman: 'He exclusively plays acoustic guitar but puts it through all sorts of effects, and it has very psychedelic textures.'

Adam Holzman, who became Wilson's regular keyboard player from the third solo album, *The Raven That Refused To Sing,* did an excellent jazz instrumental cover of this song with his band Brave New World. It's the final track on *The Last Gig,* which was recorded live in New York City on 12 March 2020, just before the first lockdown caused by the global pandemic. Holzman's version takes a slightly quieter, but equally effective approach.

'Salvaging' (8:18)

This song is divided into three sections. The first section sounds much like The Cure at their most ominous and poetic. There's a bassline with a heavy chorus pedal effect worthy of Simon Gallup of The Cure, and a lyrical guitar line of which Robert Smith, the band's guitarist, singer and main songwriter, would have been proud. Wilson, writing on Twitter, was happy to acknowledge this: 'The opening ... I guess was coming a little from The Cure's [1989 album] *Disintegration*.' The next section, lasting around two minutes, is an instrumental, with gorgeously lush orchestral string chords, arranged by Dave Gregory, played by The London Session Orchestra. Many songwriters would have ended the song with a gentle fade of these chords. Instead, there's a final section which Wilson described as 'the oppressive noise coda.' Harrison provides heavy, ominous drumming in the first section. There is some respite from the shadows in the warm string section when the drums are absent. The final section begins with epic drums, but even those become lost in the maelstrom of noise.

So why end with a burst of industrial noise? 'It was about contrasts,' Wilson said, 'taking something beautiful and stamping on it with ugliness and discord.' He was inspired by the music of Scott Walker, 'beauty and dissonance side by side.' As captured in the absorbing documentary *Scott Walker: 30 Century Man* (2006), it could be said that Walker's career began in beauty and ended in dissonance: from singing romantic ballads to punching a joint of meat to create percussion for 'Clara' (*The Drift*, 2006).

The title 'Salvaging' could refer to rescuing something or someone. Or perhaps there is an echo of the title of T.S. Eliot's poem 'The Dry Salvage' (*Four Quartets*, 1943). The title of that poem refers to a group of rocks off Rockport, Massachusetts, and in part deals with Eliot's childhood memories of living near that area. But perhaps of more relevance is the fact that Eliot wrote the poem during the air raids in London – it's easy to imagine him wearing a gas mask during the bombing, just as Wilson does on the album cover.

The song also hints at the existential angst seen in much of the art of the early to mid-20th century. In particular, the final lines – 'now the nails have been driven' – may refer to depictions of the Crucifixion in which nails are driven through Christ's hands on the cross. Iconic images include *Christ Of Saint John Of The Cross* (1951) by the Spanish surrealist artist Salvador Dalí (although Christ is obviously suspended in great anguish, there are, ironically, no nails through his hands). A more extreme version of the Crucifixion can be found in the painter Francis Bacon's 1944 triptych *Three Studies For Figures At The Base Of A Crucifixion,* which doesn't even include the figure of Christ but instead three horrific, nightmarish creatures, part-human and part-animal. The final 'noise' section of the song would make a fitting soundtrack for either of these works of art. Wilson has expressed his love of Surrealism, and the track 'Rainy Taxi' from the 1994 Porcupine Tree album *Staircase Infinities* was inspired by a 1938 Salvador Dalí art installation of the same name.

The Belgian composer and instrumentalist Dirk Serries provides guitar drones on this track and 'Get All You Deserve'. He's recorded ambient music under the name Vidna Obmana, and his other projects include Fear Falls

Burning and the Microphonics project. He's a leading figure on the Belgian jazz improv scene.

'Veneno Para Las Hadas' (5:18)

The title of the song, which means 'Poison For The Fairies', comes from a mid-1980s Mexican horror film. The Director, Carlos Enrique Taboada, was born in Mexico City, and the song was one of the first on the album to be inspired by Wilson's time there. The title relates to the final lines of the song, 'poison for a fairy', which appears to have come from the 'bottle not for sharing', a bottle of poison.

The song begins with pensive, heavily chorused guitar chords and elegant, sparse piano played by Jordan Rudess, keyboard player of American progressive metal band Dream Theater. The style is almost jazzy, similar to that of David Bowie's virtuosic keyboard player Mike Garson, although less melodramatic. It has a psychedelic, spacey feel like some of the tracks on the Porcupine Tree album *The Sky Moves Sideways* (1995). On the Twitter Listening Party, Jason/ReptilianSamurai asked, 'Does anyone else get deja vu [sic] from *The Sky Moves Sideways*?' Wilson replied, 'Yes, it's the same verse chords, Am to F major 7. I probably wasn't even conscious of it at the time.' The opening guitar chords sound very similar to those on the live version of the track 'The Sky Moves Sideways' performed by Wilson (as Porcupine Tree) on the live album *We Lost The Skyline,* recorded in Orlando, Florida, in October 2007.

This is possibly one of the most straightforward songs Wilson has ever written, with very simple chord progressions. The simplicity is accentuated by the brooding, pulsing bassline played by Wilson, consisting of a single repeated note that only changes occasionally with the harmony of the song. This gives a sense of stasis, very different from the lively, complex, highly melodic basslines of the two main players Wilson has worked with over the years, Colin Edwin in Porcupine Tree and Nick Beggs during his solo career. Wilson can play bass to an accomplished level – he has often written virtuosic lines for the players just mentioned – so his decision to write such a minimalist line is clearly deliberate. It gives the song a sense of melancholy, making it almost lugubrious, and Wilson's wistful vocals add to this. The gentle pulsing of the bassline also relates to the line 'to the pulse you're breathing'.

Wilson's vocals use a technique developed by Stockport rock band 10cc. As he said on Twitter, 'I also sampled my voice singing 'aahs' and faded notes in and out to create the chord movements (like [10cc] famously did on 'I'm Not In Love').' He's referring to the single taken from their 1975 album *The Original Soundtrack*. It reached number one in the UK and number two in the US. Wilson would have been able to sample his voice quickly and easily and then manipulate it by playing different notes on a keyboard. In the 1970s, digital technology wasn't available, so members of 10cc spent three weeks recording their voices, creating an analogue tape loop for each note of the chromatic scale. By playing all the tapes at once and raising the faders for each tape, any chord could be created in real time by members of the band at the mixing desk. Minimal instrumentation was added, and the whole song is based around the voices, creating a unique sound.

On Twitter, Wilson said that the guitar sound was based on the 'big cloud' created by bands like the American ambient duo Stars of the Lid and the Icelandic post-rock band Sigur Rós: 'Basically, you set up a big chain of delay and reverb effects so that anything you play balloons out into an ethereal wash of sound.' He also referenced the song 'Saint' from the 2006 album *Solace* by the New Zealand post-rock band Jakob. Both songs share a sombre, almost mournful feel. To add to the effect, subtle instrumental soundscaping is provided by Theo Travis on clarinet, Harrison on cymbals and Snowman on recorders.

'No Twilight Within The Courts Of The Sun' (8:37)

Wilson said on Twitter that the title 'No Twilight Within The Courts Of The Sun' was taken from the supernatural poem by Samuel Taylor Coleridge, 'The Rime Of The Ancient Mariner' (1798): 'I loved the phrase and had it written down in a notebook for a long time waiting for a song to give it to.' He may have remembered hearing the words spoken at the end of Part I of the 1975 album *The Rime Of The Ancient Mariner* by David Bedford, the English composer and musician. (Wilson said the album was a strong influence on the track 'I May Be Some Time' on the compilation *Tape Experiments 1985/1986*.) The Coleridge poem tells the story of a Mariner who shot an albatross, which his fellow sailors forced him to wear around his neck in penance: hence the metaphor of an albatross around one's neck as a heavy burden. The words of the song title are taken not from the poem itself but from the gloss that Coleridge added in 1817. The ghostly figures of Death and Life-in-Death throw dice for the souls of the sailors. Death wins the sailors' souls, and Life-in-Death wins the soul of the Mariner, condemning him to wander the earth forever, while his shipmates die:

> No twilight within the courts of the Sun
> At the rising of the Moon
> One after another
> His shipmates drop down dead

The track is in 21/8 time, which gives it a distinctive stop-start feel. In May 2011, Harrison told Bernhard Castiglioni's *Drummerworld* forum: 'I counted like this: two bars of 4/4, plus one quarter note and then two dotted eighth notes.' (In eighth notes/quavers: two bars of 4/4 = 16, one quarter note is two and two dotted eighth notes is three. Total beats = 21.) Wilson's comment on Twitter was, 'I'm not sure how a lesser drummer would have coped.' Another well-known track in a similarly unusual time signature is the opening of Mike Oldfield's *Tubular Bells* (1973). Its offbeat, unsettling piano motif made it the ideal theme tune for the 1973 film *The Exorcist*. As Oldfield told Helen Brown of *The Telegraph* in March 2014, 'That curious little figure at the beginning is in 15/8. It's like a puzzle with a little bit missing. That's why it sticks in the brain.'

After the simple bassline of the previous track, Tony Levin provides a much more complex line. Levin had toured North America with his band as a support act for Porcupine Tree. A prolific session musician, he's best known for his work with Peter Gabriel and King Crimson. The experimental influence of the latter band can be heard on this track. It's the longest track on the album, and it begins with a long instrumental section which forms almost half the song. Ed Sanders says the track starts 'very jazzy with that dissonant King Crimson style' with 'almost four minutes of fiddling around and another noisy climax.' Another way of describing this section would be a series of jazz improvisations on guitar and drums over a repeating bassline. Each drum and guitar part is different from the last, which can be either exhilarating or irritating depending on your point of view. The first guitar solo is played by Wilson himself, spiky and stylish at the same time. The second solo is played by Mike Outram, a jazz player who played guitar in The Theo Travis Quartet. His solo is astonishing, skittering wildly across the fretboard. Wilson told 'Deadwing' that Mike provided some 'insanely speedy guitar runs.'

When the vocals finally enter, they are at first almost whispered, gradually increasing in volume as the track proceeds until they are almost shouted. It's perhaps the most compelling vocal performance on the album, creating a chilling sense of a neo-noir detective movie opening with the words 'dragging a lake', reminiscent of the line in Elvis Costello's 1997 single 'Watching The Detectives', which describes the protagonist filing her nails while the police drag the lake for a body. It's difficult to follow what the rest of the words mean, but the music creates its own images in the mind.

After the explosive vocal climax, there's another instrumental section, which provides a welcome sense of release, a gorgeous free-flowing passage with sparkling, liquid keyboards and a graceful bassline. Sanders describes this as a 'delightful piece of music', and perceptively calls it a '[Porcupine] Tree-like atmospheric intermezzo.' Rudess provides what Wilson on Twitter called 'some really flowery piano', channelling Mike Garson on David Bowie's 1972 album *Aladdin Sane*. As Wilson said, 'It should be really hard to play fast over changes in 21 time, but Jordan did it like it was nothing!' Cascading showers of piano motifs gradually fade into echo with distorted guitars and electronics, and there is a short gap as the track seems to have ended. An unexpected reprise of the main bass theme from the first half of the song crashes into the silence with fierce unison guitar and bass and frenetic double kick drumming until the track grinds to a halt, with the sound of an analogue tape coming to a stop. The track is another example of combining the melodic with industrial noise.

'Significant Other' (4:32)

On Twitter, Wilson called this song 'The Cocteau Twins one!', referencing the Scottish indie rock band who combined Liz Fraser's ethereal vocals with Robin Guthrie's effects-laden guitars. Wilson tried to get Fraser as a guest vocalist: 'In a way, I'm glad it didn't happen, as it would have been too obvious.' Instead, he chose the Irish singer Clodagh Simonds (credited as 'Simmonds'), who sang on Mike Oldfield's albums *Hergest Ridge* (1974) and *Ommadawn* (1975) and, much later, formed her own band, Fovea Hex. Wilson told 'Deadwing' that he's been a big fan of hers since he heard her sing on *Ommadawn*: 'She's an incredible singer and her projects in Fovea Hex just totally blew me away.' On Twitter, he described her as an 'existential Kate Bush.' Wilson has released the band's music on his Headphone Dust label. On this track, her voice can be heard duetting with Wilson's, sometimes like a ghostly shadow of his voice, at other times intertwining and weaving in and out. Sometimes her voice takes flight on its own, soaring into the ether with a beautiful, almost spiritual quality. Her wordless melisma is similar to that of Liz Fraser. When she does sing words, they are not in a made-up language like those of Cocteau Twins but have a similar effect, surreal and deliberately impenetrable.

The Cocteau Twins influence can also be heard in the guitar sound. As Wilson said on Twitter, 'Lots of major 7 chords and effect-heavy guitar sounds on this one as per Robin Guthrie's approach.' The effects begin with a heavy chorus effect of the type often used by Robert Smith, and later heavy distortion is applied as the song becomes more epic and takes on a majestic quality. Wilson's voice is buried deep in the mix, becoming more of a texture than a clear vocal line. Tony Levin provides a subtle and inventive bassline, whose syncopated flow contrasts with the slowly evolving guitar motifs.

The song ends with Wilson playing the main chord sequence quietly on glockenspiel, a moment of intimacy after the hurricane of sound that precedes it. Although the instrument is played, it sounds here like a mechanical musical box.

'Only Child' (4:24)

On Twitter, Wilson said this track 'may be the sleeper track on the album, I'm super proud of it. I love the hypnotic quality and the drum sound.' He said the main riff is played on 'several overdubbed bass guitars', and the combination of instruments gives an effect like a chorus pedal, as the instruments go slightly in and out of phase with each other. It's also possible that an actual chorus effect is being used. However the sound is created, it's very characteristic of the tone used by two of the greatest English post-punk bass guitarists, Peter Hook (Joy Division) and Simon Gallup (The Cure). These two musicians have created some of the most memorable and melodic basslines in songs such as 'Love Will Tear Us Apart' (Joy Division, 1980), 'Pictures Of You' and 'Fascination Street' (The Cure, 1990 and 1989). 'Only

Child' fits well into such illustrious company, its repeated melodic basslines creating a mesmeric quality. Wilson's voice is quite low in the mix and unusually low in his vocal range. This helps create an atmosphere of darkness and sepulchral mystery, heightened by the almost impenetrable lyrics.

Wilson is credited with playing piano, which seems strange as the song is dominated by guitar tones. A careful listen reveals a repeated piano note at around 90 seconds in, similar to the repeated piano notes that were used in early rock 'n' roll songs such as 'Great Balls Of Fire' (1957) by Jerry Lee Lewis. But the piano in 'Only Child' couldn't be more different, creating an unchanging foil against which the guitar melodies are offset, making them appear more ominous and far from the rock 'n' roll tropes.

The voice at the end of the track is that of the Mexican photographer Susana Moyaho, who is seen a lot in the *Insurgentes* documentary. She's a member of the Mexican experimental group Pig, who appear in the documentary playing live with Wilson. The song ends with a short solo flourish from Harrison, whose drumming throughout the song is as muscular and imaginative as ever.

'Twilight Coda' (3:25)

This short track features a surprising number of guests, considering it's essentially an ambient instrumental – Outram on electric guitar, Snowman on acoustic guitar (normal and processed) and Rudess on piano. This makes more sense when the title is considered – it was originally part of 'No Twilight Within The Courts Of The Sun' but its inclusion in that song would have made it too long in Wilson's view, at around 12 minutes. As he said on Twitter, 'it became 'an instrumental 'breathing space' reprise." The only two of Wilson's distinguished guests who appeared on the main song but not on this short coda are Levin and drummer Harrison – Wilson himself and Snowman appear on percussion here.

Ed Sanders perceptively makes a link between this instrumental and the free-form ambient improvisations of Porcupine Tree's album *Metanoia,* released ten years earlier, and even further back to 'traces of the atmosphere on *Moonloop*' (1994). David Baird, in the same *DPRP* roundtable review, refers to the possible influence of French ambient band Nouvelles Lectures Cosmopolites, whose tagline on the Discogs website is 'music for romantic people: piano, concrete sounds from the wood', and the comparison is a fair one. Both critics are unsure whether the track really earns its place on the album, although Sanders does concede that it's a 'nice breather'. The track doesn't really stand on its own, but as part of a sequence, it works well.

'Get All You Deserve' (6:17)

This song provides the title for Wilson's first live solo DVD, released four years later. It was the first song he wrote for the record and marked a major change of direction from his work with Porcupine Tree. As he said on Twitter, 'it was pointing towards something very different from what I was known for with the use of pure noise.' The sleeve notes for the original album credit him with playing 'noises'. The track begins with a subtle soundscape of white noise, very different from the aggressive noise that comes later. It appears to be a gentle, melancholic piano ballad with a series of very evocative chords over which Wilson sings with an intimate, fragile tone. There's a particularly haunting and unexpected key change at around 1:13, where a chord of F major pivots into a chord of F# minor around a central A that remains the same in both chords. The heavily echoed piano is joined by warm guitar drones provided by Serries, adding to the mournful soundscape, and by Harrison's minimalist drumming. Sampled backing vocals, similar to the 10cc-inspired vocals used in 'Veneno Para Las Hadas', add to the growing richness of the sonic palette. There's even a touch of glockenspiel very low in the mix. At just over 3:00, the track seems to settle for a little while on a chord, sounding briefly very much like the chords on 10cc's 'I'm Not In Love'. After a minute or so of quiet stasis, marred only by some slightly ominous guitar sounds, the gradual and somehow inexorable descent into a cacophony of industrial noise begins at around 4:00. The drumming becomes more vigorous and tries to maintain a beat but eventually gives up as it's swamped by noise. A lone guitar tries to establish a melody but only gets as far as a rising series of notes, the first three notes of the major scale of D, but it, too, soon gives up hope. The track ends in pure noise, and very suddenly – just like the end of The Beatles' 'I Want You (She's So Heavy)' from *Abbey Road* (1969). 'Get All You Deserve' also shares, in some ways, that track's brutal emotional directness.

Wilson has often talked about his love of cinema, and many of his songs are beautiful, self-contained cinematic miniatures. On this track, he uses a very compressed format to create a narrative arc. He told 'Jeff' of *MetalStorm* that in movies, we're used to seeing the movement from a 'very happy and calm' scene to something 'quite violent that destroys the mood'. He described the fact that a ballad is 'obliterated by complete noise' as a 'very cinematic idea.' And to 'Deadwing', he said that 'the idea of sound design to stimulate emotions and feelings is something very close to my heart.' The song feels very personal, and also an important statement of intent that he no longer wanted to be part of a four-piece rock band but to be an independent solo artist.

'Insurgentes' (3:55)

The title track was written and recorded 'live' on the night of 28 February 2008 in Ex Templo de Santa Teresa La Antigua, Mexico City, during the filming of the *Insurgentes* documentary. On Twitter, Wilson said writing a song while being filmed should have been difficult, but 'on this occasion, it just clicked.' He later rerecorded the piano on a better instrument.

The only other instrumentalist on this track is the Japanese koto player Michiyo Yagi, who plays a 17-string bass. Wilson told Bennett that she's an incredible player who worked with the American composer and saxophonist John Zorn, and is 'very much part of the avant-garde jazz scene.' As a fan of The Cure, Wilson may have been familiar with the sound of the koto from 'Kyoto Song' from their 1985 album *The Head On The Door*. On that song, the sound was created by the Yamaha DX7 synthesiser, which did a remarkable impression of the instrument, but the sound of the real instrument, played by a real human being, is much richer.

It might be thought that by ending the album with what is essentially a solo track with just voice and piano (and koto), Wilson was firmly establishing himself as a solo artist. But he had done this before, while still a member of Porcupine Tree, on another beautiful piano ballad, 'Collapse The Light Into Earth', which brought the band's 2002 album *In Absentia* to a thoughtful and reflective close. Ending an album with a quiet ballad has become almost a trope for Steven, continuing even up to the final track of 'Count Of Unease' from his sixth album, *The Future Bites,* and encompassing perhaps the most famous example, the title track of *The Raven That Refused To Sing,* with which he has often ended his live performances.

Grace For Drowning (2011)

Personnel:
Steven Wilson: vocals, keys, guitars, autoharp, bass guitar, percussion, piano, gong, glockenspiel, programming, harmonium
Jordan Rudess: piano
Theo Travis: saxophone, clarinet, flute
Ben Castle: clarinet on 'Sectarian'
Nick Beggs: Chapman stick, bass guitar
Tony Levin: bass guitar
Steve Hackett: guitar on 'Remainder The Black Dog'
Pat Mastelotto: electronic drums on 'No Part Of Me' and 'Index'
Trey Gunn: guitar and bass on 'No Part Of Me'
Markus Reuter: guitar on 'No Part Of Me'
Mike Outram: guitar on 'Raider II'
London Session Orchestra: strings
Nic France: drums
Synergy Vocals: choir
Recorded at No Man's Land, Hemel Hempstead, Koolworld, Luton, Angel Studios, Islington, between January 2010 and June 2011
Steven Wilson: production, mixing
Dave Stewart: string and choir arrangements
Release date: September 2011
Highest chart placings: UK: 34, US: 85
Running time: 83:01
Record label: Kscope
Current edition: Kscope
Grammy-nominated for Best Surround Sound Album 2012: Steven Wilson: engineer/producer, Paschal Byrne: mastering engineer
Dedication: 'to my father, Michael George Wilson – 1938 – 2011, without whom ...'

Grace For Drowning is Steven Wilson's second solo album, released in 2011. The meaning of the album's unusual title is mysterious. 'Grace' could refer to the lighthouse keeper's daughter, Grace Darling. In 1838, she became a national hero when she and her father saved nine crew members from the shipwrecked *Forfarshire* from drowning, near the Farne Islands off the coast of Northumberland.

Wilson has spoken very rarely about the title. In August 2011, he told Stephen Humphries of *PopMatters* that it came from descriptions of people who had suffered near-death experiences when they almost drowned. They all said that 'they got to a point where they stopped struggling, where they reached a point of calm, of grace.' An example of this, quoted in an article by Christof Koch in *Scientific American* in June 2020, is the 'calm feeling of the most perfect tranquillity' experienced by Admiral Sir Francis Beaufort, who nearly drowned in 1791. These may be spiritual experiences, but Koch, taking a rigorous scientific approach, concludes that the reason why the brain experiences loss of oxygen as 'positive and blissful rather than as panic-inducing remains mysterious.'

Wilson rather poignantly told Humphries that he saw this state of grace as a 'metaphor for my life.' He was no longer worried about success: 'I'd still like to share my music with more people. But I'm not stressed about it.' Wilson had been thinking deeply about this for a long time. On Porcupine Tree's *Stupid Dream* (1999), Wilson contrasts his teenage dream of becoming a rock star with the harsh reality of being a musician when music can become a commodity rather than art. In 2000, during the sessions for *Lightbulb Sun,* he recorded the gorgeous song 'Buying New Soul' (released on *Recordings* in 2001) in which he movingly describes his fight with the music industry – 'I still rage and wage my little war' – but ends up feeling he has sold out, being forced to 'buy a new soul' every year. And one of the themes of the 1996 Porcupine Tree album *Signify* is the attempt to make something significant out of one's life.

By 2011, he told Humphries he'd reached a kind of equilibrium, an acceptance of his position, 'I'm making the best music I've ever made now because I feel totally liberated from trying to please anyone.' But elsewhere, he expressed his frustration at being ignored by the mainstream media. He told Graham Reid of *Elsewhere Magazine* in September 2011 that 'one of the big newspapers here [in England] wouldn't review my album because I was too under the radar … this is partly their ignorance but also a wilful laziness.'

In 2012, he told Anil Prasad of *Innerviews* his ambition was to 'eclipse everything that I had done before, including Porcupine Tree', particularly in his live shows. He wanted to avoid the impression that his solo work was a side project. He didn't want his work to be 'stripped down 'Steven Wilson with his piano and acoustic guitar' efforts.'

A specific limitation of Porcupine Tree, as he told Steven Rosen of *Ultimate-Guitar.com*, was that 'I know for a fact in Porcupine Tree, one of the guys hates jazz.' He told Grant Moon of *Prog* magazine in September 2011 that it's easy to forget the role jazz played in the birth of prog rock: 'It was when pop musicians started to incorporate their love of jazz and classical that progressive emerged.' He referred to Bill Bruford, who played with Yes and King Crimson but was a jazz drummer at heart, and to King Crimson co-founders Michael Giles and Ian McDonald, who 'both grew up listening to jazz and chose to form a rock 'n' roll band [with Robert Fripp, Greg Lake, and Peter Sinfield].'

In April 2012, Wilson told Thodoris of *Hit Channel (Greece)* that *Grace For Drowning* was the first time he had incorporated jazz elements into his songwriting: 'I think on this album, I'm not interested only in jazz; it has all sides of my musical taste … the only thing actually I hadn't done before is writing jazz.' As he told Rosen, he brought in jazz musicians because he didn't feel able to improvise: 'That's something that's been lacking for me in a lot of my work over the last ten years ...'

Wilson chose jazz drummer Nic France as he wanted 'a very different approach to drumming than a rock drummer would take.' He also invited two other jazz musicians – flautist and saxophonist Theo Travis and guitarist Mike Outram, who had both played on *Insurgentes*. He told Prasad that he recorded fairly elaborate demos for the album, as was his usual practice, but this time, he 'allowed a lot more space for accidents ... the soloists had the opportunity to express themselves without the restrictions of tight arrangements.' The most obvious example of this freedom is 'Raider II', which includes Theo Travis' long solos. He felt that these passages were 'spiritual', in the sense that they came 'directly from the heart or soul.'

Wilson also changed his approach to recording. He was of the generation who grew up recording into a computer, meticulously overdubbing each part, asking the drummer to play to a click track so that the tempo didn't drift. When he was asked to remix classic albums by King Crimson and Jethro Tull in 5.1 surround sound, he was amazed to discover that those bands and others from the 1960s and 1970s recorded in a completely different way. He told Rosen that by going back to the original master tapes, he learned how the records were made, by 'going into the studio with a band and just setting up and playing as a group.' He adopted this approach on several of the tracks on *Grace For Drowning*, with bass, guitar, drums, sax and flute all played live in the studio. This didn't work on all the tracks – for instance, 'Deform To Form A Star' was too complicated. But tracks like 'Sectarian', 'Remainder The Black Dog' and big parts of the epic 'Raider II' were 'cut live in the studio.' Later, he told Prasad that the live versions of the songs were even better: 'No matter how pleased you are with what you do in the studio ... a great group of musicians can prove you wrong time and time again. And they did prove me wrong, every night.'

At just over 80 minutes, the album is perhaps just too long to fit on a single CD. Originally, CDs were designed to be no more than 74 minutes, but their length has crept up slightly over the years. Roger Trenwith of *DPRP* said in September 2011 that Wilson had made a virtue of having to split the album into two, giving the listener a break and 'a chance to indulge in a metaphorical half-time orange.' The two CDs have their own names, taken from tracks on each CD. Volume I is 'Deform To Form A Star' and Volume II is 'Like Dust I Have Cleared From My Eye'.

The cover depicts Wilson seen from behind in silhouette against the setting sun. The image has a vivid orange glow like an oil painting, although it is, in fact, a photograph taken by Lasse Hoile. It bears a striking resemblance to a painting by the German 19th-century Romantic landscape painter Caspar David Friedrich called *Woman Before The Rising Sun* (also known as *Woman Before The Setting Sun*), which shows a woman from behind silhouetted against a bright orange sky. The painting is in the Museum Folkwang, Essen, Germany. Wilson told Thodoris that Hoile used an analogue camera – which may explain the painterly look – and took the photo 'at the very last moments of the daylight … that time the sun is getting very red and orange … it was like twilight.'

Vol 1 – Deform To Form A Star

'Grace For Drowning' (2:00)

The title track is the shortest on the album. It features 40 tracks of gorgeously rich wordless vocals, which sometimes sound like the Beach Boys, for whose work Wilson has expressed his admiration. The lack of a clear rhythmic pulse creates a sense of resignation to drowning, a gentle feeling of grace.

Jordan Rudess adds piano, limpid and quicksilver, impressionistic like French composer Debussy in his *Preludes* (1910 and 1913) and *Children's Corner* (1908) for solo piano. A Debussy piece that may spring to mind is 'The Snow Is Dancing', which was given full prog credentials in a remarkable electronic version by Japanese synth pioneer Isao Tomita on his poetic album *Snowflakes Are Dancing* (1974).

'Sectarian' (7:45)

As this is an instrumental track and the opener featuring wordless vocals, it's a good ten minutes into the album before we hear Wilson singing lyrics. This feels like a very deliberate attempt to move away from his role as lead singer of Porcupine Tree. As Roger Trenwith of *DPRP* said in September 2011, this track has 'just the right amount of jazz smokiness in between the heavier passages', immediately establishing the album's 'jazz-prog' credentials. Wilson provides crunchy acoustic guitar chords that open the track, and the distorted guitar lines that appear later. He also supplies the distinctive Mellotron choir motif that foreshadows the use of a real choir (Synergy Vocals) later on the album. He plays the free-flowing and jazzy electric piano that appears at around four minutes in.

Travis plays invigorating, free-form jazz on saxophone, very different from the mellifluous solos more familiar to rock fans on tracks like 'Money' and 'Us And Them' by Pink Floyd (performed by Dick Parry on *The Dark Side Of The Moon,* 1973). France provides loose-limbed jazz drumming, more laid-back than Gavin Harrison's work on the previous album, *Insurgentes*.

At the end of the track, there is a short clarinet solo from Ben Castle, simple but haunting. He's the younger son of jazz trumpeter Roy Castle, best known to the British public as presenter of the television show *Record Breakers*.

'Deform To Form A Star' (8:00)

Like the title track, this song begins with flowing piano in an almost classical style from Rudess. On Wilson's 2013 tour, keyboard player Adam Holzman performed a different version every night, only keeping the first few bars the same. That same year, Holzman released an album called *The Deform Variations*, made up of 27 different improvisations recorded live across the world. On the Bandcamp website, Holzman wrote, 'I would like to tip my hat to Jordan

Rudess, who performed the original intro … I use that as a starting point. All of these pieces, with the exception of those first few bars, are improvised.'

Porcupine Tree fans may feel on more familiar ground with this style of song, in particular the gorgeously rich backing vocals in the chorus. The Porcupine Tree song 'Stars Die' from the mid-1990s also has a star-based theme. But whereas the earlier song is about the death of humanity, the title 'Deform To Form A Star' song has a more hopeful message, suggesting that out of the destruction of a star, a new star can grow.

On *SongMeanings.com* in July 2012, Bandita provided an astute analysis, which is both scientific and poetic:

> I think it's a great analogy between stars and relationships. When a star is dying, the blown-off outer layers include elements which may be recycled during new star formation ... when we start a relationship, we die a little to create something that we thought could be beautiful.

After the introduction, the track stops briefly to gather itself, then the piano ballad begins again. Wilson's vocals in the verse are very close-mic'd, intimate and confessional. A rising, optimistic four-note theme leads into the chorus as the song opens out with multi-layered backing vocals. The use of Mellotron chords in the chorus gives the song a nostalgic feel, tinged with melancholy. The song is immediately attractive and accessible, and Wilson chose a slightly cut-down version for his 2015 compilation album *Transience*, an introduction to 'the more accessible side of his music.'

'No Part Of Me' (5:45)

In his book, *Limited Edition Of One* (2022), Wilson lists this song and the next song, 'Postcard', as two of his top five 'most depressing songs I have ever written.' It features some of Wilson's most brutal lyrics, about the end of a relationship built on 'security' rather than true love: 'There's no part of me in you'. The protagonist has reached such a weary point in life that it's no use drinking alcohol, as that wouldn't help. He's on the edge of the state of grace that drowning can bring, but is unable to reach it. His life has slowed 'right down', but he's still held above the water, unable to resign himself to its sweet embrace – life still holds him 'above the water line', and he is unable, metaphorically, to submit himself to death: 'sleep will never come.'

The track begins with the twinkling of an electronic music box, with a single bass drum and busy percussion. It's almost two minutes before the vocals appear, and the opening words – 'I feel worn out' – suggest that the protagonist finds it difficult even to summon up the energy to sing. Wilson's vocal delivery is appropriately weary. Trenwith correctly describes the 'rampant cynicism' of the song. Yet, there's a certain fragile beauty as strings from the London Session Orchestra join at about 2:00, with a touch of muted sax that sounds like Miles Davis's trumpet.

The vocalist soon loses momentum, giving up altogether halfway through the song, leaving a long instrumental outro. The guitar solo is played by German guitarist Markus Reuter, known for his guitar tapping technique, similar to the style used by Nick Beggs on the Chapman Stick. Reuter has developed his own guitars under the Touch name. Each guitar has eight or ten strings as opposed to the usual six, and tapping is done with both hands at once using all eight fingers. Here, he plays his own U8 model. Trey Gunn plays a Warr touch guitar designed for single or double-handed playing. Beggs plays the bass solo. The instrumental section of the song evokes Middle Eastern melodies at times as the song gains urgency, despite the deeply melancholy theme. Like many Porcupine Tree songs, it has a completely unconventional structure, with two verses bunched together near the middle of the song and no chorus. Even the lyrics refuse to follow conventional rhythms, creating almost a stream of consciousness.

'Postcard' (4:30)
This track picks up the lyrical theme from the previous song. The protagonist is again searching for sleep as a way to avoid the realities of his life following a breakup: 'I better sleep while life is so mundane'. He's left completely bereft: 'all that matters disappeared when I lost you'.

Wilson has generally been very guarded about his private life – quite rightly so – but he has occasionally mentioned with great bitterness a relationship that left a very deep scar when it ended. Some of the lyrics he wrote for Porcupine Tree's 2009 album *The Incident* refer to this relationship ending. In November 2009, in a YouTube interview for his record label, Roadrunner, he described the extreme emotions he felt about his former lover, who he felt had cast a shadow across his life. This is expressed in songs like 'Bonnie The Cat' and 'Remember Me Lover', whose lyrics are deeply unpleasant.

Whether the two breakup songs on *Grace For Drowning* are inspired by the same events is unclear, but in some ways, it doesn't matter, as they share a raw, emotional truth, giving them a universal quality. This song describes someone who has reached the lowest point possible. There's a chilling vision at the end of the song when the protagonist is viewed by others as the tragic person, 'the one you always seem to read about'. This presumably refers to the character's suicide or a similar tragic event, although it's not made explicit.

The song is based around a sequence of simple piano chords, pivoting around C major and E minor at the start. Lush strings are provided by the London Session Orchestra, arranged by Dave Stewart. A wordless choir, members of Synergy Vocals, join at around 3.00. Wilson told Humphries he'd aimed for an 'almost over the top' sound from the choir: 'It's almost like a Hollywood moment. Sickly sweet.' He was no longer frightened of being 'a little bit kitsch', even if that meant being accused of being pompous or pretentious. The richness of the arrangement creates a cognitive dissonance with the utterly bleak subject matter, almost mocking the protagonist, perhaps suggesting he is being self-indulgent in the depths of his depression.

'Raider Prelude' (2:30)

This short instrumental track prefigures some of the horrors of the epic 'Raider II' on the second half of the album. It begins with wordless singing from Synergy Vocals. The shifting harmonies sound like a late Romantic composer, such as the Austrian composer Anton Bruckner, who wrote several acapella motets in a similar style. Another, more contemporary reference (picked up by Daren Epperson on YouTube in 2016) is the American choral music composer Eric Whitacre (born in 1970).

About halfway through, a mysterious piano motif appears, a simple falling fifth low in the piano's register. Although the interval of a fifth is called the perfect fifth because it's neutral, neither major nor minor, it sounds eerie in this context, with dissonant voices swirling around it. To complete the feeling of music for a horror film, the track ends with the shimmering of a gong.

'Remainder The Black Dog' (9:30)

The closing track on Disc One adopts the metaphor of the 'black dog' used by Winston Churchill to describe the depression he suffered, although the first recorded use of the term dates back to the writer Samuel Johnson in the late 18th century.

The word 'remainder' in the title suggests all that's left for the protagonist is depression, and the imagery of the song is all about paranoia, neuroses and prescription pills, which are ignored. The final lines of the song are ambiguous: 'If you would dare to dissolve/You'd get the thing that you craved for so long now'. On *Genius.com*, Georgi Shumkov suggests that this refers to 'acceptance of death', but dissolving could also refer to self-destruction in the form of suicide.

Most of the song is a complex, jazz-prog instrumental. It begins with a repeated piano riff played by Wilson, which becomes a musical motif for much of the song, creating a claustrophobic atmosphere that matches the heavily compressed vocals. Wilson also plays a funky, distorted electric piano. Later in the track, from around 5:35, he uses a sparkling synth patch in the style of his Porcupine Tree bandmate Richard Barbieri, providing texture rather than virtuosic soloing.

From around 3:45, Travis plays a sax solo in the style of David Jackson of Van der Graaf Generator, frenetic, angular and disturbed, adding to the unsettled feeling of the track. And there's another link to that band, in the occasional driving, pulsating, repeated proggy riff (for instance at 4:25), very characteristic of Van der Graaf's style on tracks like 'A Plague Of Lighthouse Keepers' from *Pawn Hearts* (1971). Steve Hackett provides guitar parts. Wilson told Moon that he met Hackett (guitarist with Genesis from 1970 to 1977) at the High Voltage Festival in 2010. Hackett performed on the Prog

Stage at the Festival in Victoria Park, East London. Wilson told Moon, 'I've never been a big Genesis fan, but I was a huge fan of [Hackett's] first few solo albums.' The two musicians found common ground when Hackett said he'd been inspired by King Crimson and Van der Graaf Generator, 'two touchstones' for Wilson, so 'having him on the record made perfect sense.'

The video, evocatively shot in sepia tones by Lasse Hoile, uses some of the tropes from the 'Harmony Korine' video from the previous album. A cloaked human being, this time with an animal skull and antlers, appears, and again there are birds, although this time they are real – a bird of prey and an owl. The more extreme musical passages are illustrated with moments of visceral horror.

Vol 2 – Like Dust I Have Cleared From My Eye

'Belle De Jour' (3:00)

The opening track on Disc Two. Wilson told Reid that this instrumental is a homage to European film soundtracks from the 1960s and 1970s, by composers such as Ennio Morricone and Nino Rota. What he loved about these film scores was that they 'often had almost a childlike lullaby quality to them, but there was also something sinister going on underneath.' He referenced, in particular, the theme music for Roman Polanski's psychological horror film *Rosemary's Baby* (1968), written by the Polish composer Krzysztof Komeda, in which innocent, wordless vocals, sung by the film's star, Mia Farrow, almost in the style of a French romantic comedy, sail above the sinister instruments that lurk beneath.

The title is taken from one of Wilson's favourite films, the French film *Belle De Jour* (1967), directed by the Spanish director Luis Buñuel, whose surreal work Wilson has admired elsewhere. Catherine Deneuve plays Séverine Serizy, alias Belle de Jour, a young woman who works as a high-class prostitute while her husband is at work during the day (hence the name belle de jour – a 'lady of the daytime').

Wilson plays percussive guitar parts on a nylon-strung guitar, and cinematic strings are played by the London Session Orchestra. Wilson also plays autoharp, which is reminiscent of the zither played (albeit much faster) by Anton Karas on the soundtrack to *The Third Man* (1949), adding to the film noir feeling of the track. A female voice appears around halfway through, but no singer is credited, so this is presumably a keyboard sample. The track has a timeless quality, referencing classic film soundtracks without pastiche.

Wilson told Reid it would be impossible to play the song live – 'I can't imagine how we could do that, it's all acoustic' – and he hasn't performed it live to date.

The haunting video, shot appropriately to look like an old film, features Wilson in a hotel room, then walking on a beach. It feels moody and atmospheric until a ghostly figure, wrapped in bandages, appears briefly. The understated horror continues when Wilson takes a Polaroid picture of what's in front of him, only to discover that it's himself. Finally, the ghostly figure appears on the beach, and Wilson runs away in fear.

'Index' (4:45)
Wilson said this song was inspired by a novel, just as the 2007 Porcupine Tree album *Fear Of A Blank Planet* was. In a fan forum on *StarsDie.com*, hosted by Rob Skarin, Wilson said that the album wouldn't have existed without the Bret Easton Ellis book *Lunar Park* (2005). And 'Index' probably wouldn't have existed if Wilson hadn't read *The Collector* by John Fowles, which was published in 1963, and was followed swiftly in 1965 by the film version starring Terence Stamp and Samantha Eggar. The story concerns Frederick, an amateur butterfly collector, and his unhealthy obsession with Miranda, a young art student at the Slade in London. He captures her, comparing her to a rare butterfly like a Pale Clouded Yellow, and imprisons her in his cellar.

The novel could easily have been a misogynistic thriller in which a woman plays a helpless victim to a predatory man who is only interested in sexual gratification. But the book is much more interesting than that. It explores the psychological interplay of the two protagonists from their own viewpoints. The first part is seen through Frederick's eyes, and the second part is Miranda's diaries describing the same events. Their relationship is subtly drawn, sometimes revealing a strange tenderness between captor and prisoner, and other times a deep, bitter dislike and mistrust of each other. A recurring theme is Miranda's social superiority – she sees herself as Miranda, Prospero's daughter in Shakespeare's *The Tempest* (c. 1610), and calls her captor Caliban, the monster who is Prospero's servant. This is partly a means of protecting herself from Frederick, but there's a slightly unpleasant undercurrent of snobbery, the sophisticated art student belittling the lower-middle-class man who can only afford his large house due to a recent Football Pools win.

Miranda doesn't appear in the song, although there are brief images of a woman who may be her in the video. Wilson does, however, capture Frederick's self-conscious inability to speak in what Miranda would regard as 'proper' English: 'I keep the rubbish *what* other people give away'. It's in small but significant details like this that Wilson is able to compress and crystallise a long-form work of art into a short and highly effective song.

In a fascinating analysis of the video on *The Odyssey Online* in November 2015, Alec John Simkiss of Western Carolina University says the video isn't about a killer as it might appear, but about Wilson himself. He says the mannequins that sit next to Wilson on the couch represent Wilson's side projects, including the (then) apparently disbanded Porcupine Tree. The mannequins are burned at the end of the video, showing Wilson's desire to defy expectation by not continuing the band when it was at its most successful, to be 'beyond the genres, to be his own creator and not be defined.' The dead insects that flash on the screen, collected and catalogued, represent his creativity being trapped under glass. Hands mounted on the wall represent 'the demand for another release.' Wilson's love of collecting albums is also reflected (in the *Insurgentes* DVD, Wilson says he loves to collect and file his records alphabetically and chronologically). 'Autographing' the objects he collects refers to him adding his own stamp onto classic albums by King Crimson and others that he has remixed. The hoarding of objects represents Wilson's collecting of different musical genres in his work.

Simkiss justifies his theories by saying that, by his own admission, artists like Wilson often insert parts of themselves into their work. This makes Wilson himself a 'killer', but fortunately only to the extent that he is 'killing download culture' by continuing to promote full-length albums as complete works of art. It's very convincingly argued, and much of what Simkiss says ties in with statements that Wilson has made about his career. There is perhaps an added poignancy to the words 'It isn't easy being me, it's kind of lonely work', which could apply to Wilson's own career, in which he has consistently followed his own creative path despite the risk of alienating some of his fans.

But there is a more straightforward explanation. The protagonist seems at first to be a harmless eccentric who obsessively collects things and indexes them. But there is a darker side to his personality. It's implied that he may be a murderer, even a serial killer. Lombaxianon, commenting on *SongMeanings.com* in April 2013, said, 'It's about a serial killer collecting body parts and stuff; Wilson said it himself to the audience at recent concerts.' Wilson has admitted a fascination with the inner lives of serial killers, as shown in many of the songs on Porcupine Tree's *In Absentia* (2002). In particular, 'The Creator Has A Mastertape' begins with the following lines, about another collector who *did* carry out his dark, twisted fantasies:

> He captured and collected things
> And he put them in a shed
> He raised a proper family
> So he could tie them to a bed

It's unclear whether the protagonist in 'Index' will carry out his deepest desires, addressed to an unseen victim: 'I'd collect you too if I was given half a chance/and trap you under glass'. He fantasises about putting his victim 'in a little cage' so that he can 'take you out and study you every day'. Wilson draws us into the horrific world that such protagonists inhabit, inviting us to empathise while we remain repulsed. Wilson is more interested in the psyche of serial killers than in the physical aspects of their dehumanising crimes. In *The Making Of In Absentia*, the documentary by Hoile from the 2020 Deluxe Edition, Wilson said he'd been fascinated by serial killers after finding books about them that his mother had around the house. He was trying to understand how someone could have so little empathy for other human beings that they could treat their victims 'like a toy to be used, abused and then killed and discarded.' Even though he felt no empathy for them, he was 'captivated ... by these people. They really do walk the same planet as we do.'

There is also a certain quaintness in the protagonist's language that makes him seem more human. There can't be many songs that use words like 'catalogue, preserve, amass' (also the title of Wilson's 2012 live album), 'index' and 'Rolodex' (a rotating filing system for business cards) all in the same song.

A middle ground between the above interpretations was provided by Mobman47 in January 2013 on *SongMeanings.com*, who suggests that Wilson himself is a record collector, and this is what his life might have been like 'if he compulsively *had* to buy records and his house looked like an episode of that *Hoarders* television show. Maybe he feels a little bit like he is one of those people, just a little bit more sane.' In 2014, CharMarRuleson drily added, 'This song is very creepy; victims of serial killers should avoid Steven Wilson's music in general!'

Musically, the track is a perfect miniature psychodrama or a horror film, at once intimate and epic. King Crimson drummer Pat Mastelotto opens the track with rolling, military drums, which suggest the almost military precision with which the protagonist collects and indexes objects and people. Mastelotto also plays electric drums, sometimes sounding like the objects clanking into the metal tray on which the protagonist keeps them; sometimes like the creaking of floorboards in a haunted house; and at other times played with a robotic precision that evokes the protagonist's lack of empathy.

Wilson's vocals are initially doubled by a sinister whisper, using the technique he perfected on the Porcupine Tree song 'Blackest Eyes' (*In Absentia*). Ominously, the earlier song features a man who commits terrible harm to women, and it appears that the protagonist in the later song may do the same. As the song progresses, the vocalist is joined by a crazed, distorted voice an octave higher that shows that he is descending into madness. As he does so, an ominous string motif, rising chromatically, increases the growing sense of terror and unease. Sweeping cinematic strings from the London Session Orchestra and heavy electronics bring the song to an end as radio static and an unidentified radio voice replace the strings.

'Track One' (4:15)

'Track One' is, in fact, the third track on part two of the album. It hints at the breakup of a relationship in lines like, 'The treachery of the coldness/Of your smile', but the lyrics are mostly surreal, deliberately impenetrable, only taking up about the first quarter of the song. At around a minute in, the song bursts into a joyful haze of falsetto backing vocals while a lyrical Mellotron choir provides an ethereal backdrop. But this moment of contemplative beauty is brutally shattered by a vicious onslaught of heavy drums and ominous keyboard washes. This sudden descent into noise is very similar to several of the tracks on *Insurgentes,* where a ballad is subsumed by horror. Lasse Hoile's video illustrates this transition perfectly, starting with Wilson shot almost in silhouette from the side, a lonely troubadour. A ghostly figure appears when the horror begins, holding a flare that spews out ominous red smoke.

Wilson plays the guitar solo at around 3:00. He told Steven Rosen, 'I'm no great guitar player, but I think I have a sound and a style. He modestly compared himself unfavourably to Robert Fripp (King Crimson) and Mikael Åkerfeldt (Opeth), who spend several hours a day practising. In fact, the solo would be worthy of Åkerfeldt – and even sounds rather like him.

'Raider II' (23:15)

If 'Index' hints darkly at a (serial) killer, 'Raider II' is explicit in its references. The songs on *In Absentia* that feature killers as protagonists attempt to enter the dark side of the human psyche, to see the world through their eyes. Some are loosely based on the crimes of serial killers Fred and Rosemary West. 'Raider II' is also based on a real-life serial killer, Dennis Rader, as confirmed by Wilson on his website in February 2017. The name of the song led spiraleyes (on *SongMeanings.com* in January 2013) to suggest 'raider' refers to a robber, but it seems to be a pun on Rader's name.

Rader killed ten people, two of them children, in Wichita, Kansas, between 1974 and 1991. He began by murdering Joseph and Julie Otero and two of their five children in January 1974, and went on to kill seven women. In August 2005, he was convicted of all ten murders and given ten life sentences without the possibility of parole for 40 years. Rader became known as the BTK killer, the acronym for Bind Torture Kill, which he himself created to describe his horrific modus operandi. He was an outwardly respectable citizen, defying the cliché of the serial killer as a lonely misfit. He was married with two children, was a leader at his local Lutheran church and a Scout leader. He worked briefly on an assembly line and from 1974 for a security company, ADT, as a supervisor for engineers who installed alarms. In 1991, he became a Park City compliance officer, apparently being assiduous in enforcing rules stating local residents had to keep their lawns trimmed and their dogs on leads. As well as inspiring Wilson's song, the case has had a major cultural impact. Stephen King and Thomas Harris have both written characters based on Rader. He appears in series two of the Netflix series *Mindhunter*. And Paul Spector in the BBC drama series *The Fall* is partly based on Rader.

The song sticks fairly closely to some of the facts about Rader. Cutting off the phone to prevent potential victims from calling for help is based on Rader's methods. In March 2005, Denise Mattocks, who worked with Rader at ADT, told Michael McElroy of *The New York Times* that every time she went home, she checked her phone for a dialling tone to make sure that the BTK killer hadn't cut the line. She discussed the BTK killer with Rader, but he seemed to prefer to deflect the conversation to his home life, 'his wife, the tomatoes in his garden, his Boy Scout outings.' Mattocks grimly acknowledged that the fear that the killer had instilled in the local community increased the demand for the security alarms that her company installed.

The song's protagonist checks for 'fibres between the teeth' of his victims and in the floorboards, and for fingerprints, and goes through 'the trash', presumably to remove traces of forensic evidence. Rader obtained a bachelor's degree from Wichita State University, majoring in Crime, so he may have picked up some ideas about cleaning up crime scenes. He appears to have been meticulous. According to the BBC News website, he took the body of one of his victims to his local church and spent 'about five hours cleaning up the scene before dumping her body.'

The song's protagonist says, 'Maybe I just wanted some attention', which ties in with Rader's desire for publicity. According to Monica Davey in *The New York Times* in March 2005, when the police announced they had a possible confession in one case, Rader wrote a letter expressing 'frustration that someone else might be trying to assume credit.' According to Tim Ott of *Biograpy.com* in August 2021, *The Wichita Eagle* ran a story in January 2004, marking the 30th anniversary of the first murders, and suggested that 'BTK might have moved away or even died.' Rader's indignant response was a frenzy of renewed activity after a quarter of a century of silence. He sent letters and packages to the local media, and left some in a local park, full of 'trinkets, some apparently from the killings: photographs, a word puzzle, a doll with a plastic bag over its head, a necklace, a computer disk and a victim's driver's license.' It was as a result of DNA evidence and information on the computer disk that Rader was eventually caught. According to sjstewarton on *SongMeanings.com* in May 2013, Rader 'previously [asked] the police if such a thing could be traced, and the police lied and said no.'

At just over 23 minutes, 'Raider II' was by far the longest song of Wilson's solo career, at least until he released *The Overview* (2025), which consists of two long tracks. He told Thodoris that 'the longer the musical journey is, the more chances there are to get lost ... you have to be in great form, or you will get lost.' Were it not slightly buried in a much longer jazz-prog album – or had it been released in the early 1970s – it would probably be held in as high regard as classic long tracks such as 'Close To The Edge' (Yes, *Close To The Edge,* 1972), 'Echoes' (Pink Floyd, *Meddle*, 1971), 'Supper's Ready' (Genesis, *Foxtrot,* 1972), 'A Plague Of Lighthouse Keepers' (Van der Graaf Generator, *Pawn Hearts,* 1971) or several of the tracks on *Bitches Brew* (Miles Davis, 1970). It shares with all these tracks the same epic ambition, the same variety of musical invention and artistic ambition, and the same degree of structural coherence and satisfying narrative flow.

The track begins with the ominous piano theme heard already in 'Raider Prelude', with wind textures added by Travis on flute and clarinet. Verse one appears at about 2:00. Wilson was working with Robert Fripp on a 5.1 surround sound mix of the *Lizard* (1971) by King Crimson at the time and the opening vocal line is very similar to the opening line of 'Cirkus' from that album (as is the sparkling piano part on the title track of *Grace*, which is very like the opening of 'Cirkus'). That album's use of jazz musicians, such as pianist Keith Tippett, and brass and woodwind players Robin Miller, Mark Charig, and Nick Evans, may well have had an influence on Wilson's musical direction. Around 3:00, a new 'metal' riff is introduced with added choir from Synergy Vocals – sounding, as they do elsewhere on the track, uncannily like the choir setting on a Mellotron, but with the added depth of human voices.

Verse two features an unsettling doubling of the lead vocals an octave above, the spooky upper voice eventually taking the lead line on its own. From about 4:00, the track goes into full jazz mode, with first a fluttering flute joining the metal riff, and a florid jazz piano solo from Jordan Rudess. At 7.00, a scratchy trip-hop drum pattern introduces verse three.

A minute later, the metal theme returns, but this time there is full prog-jazz improvisation, like King Crimson in full flight. A dark, film noir section follows at around 9:30, with a repeated bassline played by Nick Beggs (his first appearance on a Steven Wilson album) while Travis provides a sax solo. At 11:00, frenetic guitar chords lead to a return of the main riff, after which explosive, distorted guitar chords are detonated. A spacey, psychedelic section leads to a return of the opening piano motif. At 14:30, there's a section with pure electronic sounds, spacious drumming, acoustic guitar arpeggios and a dreamlike solo flute.

Verse four introduces a new melody, with the words 'I'm Raider', which the protagonist repeats like a badge of honour. At 17:30, Wilson, having taken over from Beggs, provides a distorted bass solo. A new, repeated guitar sequence leads to what appears to be the final section of the song, another dystopian King Crimson-style metal riff with wailing saxes, which grinds to an inevitable halt with final drum flourishes.

The short outro features eerie sound design by American musician Dave Kerzner, one of the early pioneers of sampling technology, creating sound libraries of real instruments. A lonely, desolate-sounding jazz guitar solo by Mike Outram is followed by a metallic clang of percussion, marking the true end of the track.

'Like Dust I Have Cleared From My Eye' (8:00)

After the virtuosic onslaught of 'Raider II', this gentle ballad is a moment of release with which to end the album. The simple chorus, repeating the words 'Breathe in now, breathe out loud' is similar to that of another ballad that ends an album, 'Glass Arm Shattering' – 'Feeling are you touching/Feeling all your love' – from the 2005 Porcupine Tree album *Deadwing*.

The track feels almost like a love song at first in its simple balladry, but it soon becomes clear that it's quite a bitter breakup song. It opens with the protagonist's former lover laughing at him, but he predicts that she will soon find herself suffering 'the same situation, the same disappointment you bring'.

The protagonist is able to distance himself sufficiently from his former lover that he can now regard her as a mere speck of dust he's removed from his eye, something minor and insignificant that no longer troubles him. This imagery may remind some readers of the Biblical parable of the Mote and the Beam, which was part of Jesus' discourse known as the Sermon on the Mount. In that parable, the hypocrite is so concerned with tiny faults in others – the 'mote' or speck of dust in the other person's eye – that he fails to see his own major faults, the 'beam' or huge piece of wood in his own eye.

It's unclear whether the song is personal to Wilson himself. As mentioned above, he had previously spoken about a very damaging breakup. If it is about the same relationship, then he has clearly moved on, 'your words have no meaning'. He is now able to forget her, and to stare serenely 'up at the sky'. The second half of the track depicts him doing just that, with tranquil synth soundscapes that are a little like early Tangerine Dream, a peaceful end to a musically complex album.

The Raven That Refused to Sing (And Other Stories) (2013)

Personnel:
Steven Wilson: lead vocals, Mellotron, keyboards, guitars, bass guitar on 'The Holy Drinker'
Guthrie Govan: lead guitar
Nick Beggs: bass guitar, Chapman Stick on 'The Holy Drinker', backing vocals
Adam Holzman: Fender Rhodes, Hammond organ, piano, Minimoog
Marco Minnemann: drums, percussion
Theo Travis: flute, saxophone, clarinet
Jakko Jakszyk: additional vocals on 'Luminol' and 'The Watchmaker'
Alan Parsons: haw-haw guitar on 'The Holy Drinker'
London Session Orchestra: strings, arranged by Dave Stewart
Recorded at East West Studios, Los Angeles, September 2012, No Man's Land, Hemel Hempstead, between January and July and October 2012, Angel Studio (strings) in October 2012
Produced and mixed by Steven Wilson
Associate producer: Alan Parsons
Release date: February 2013
Chart placings: UK: 28, US: 57
Running time: 54:43
Record label: Kscope
Award: Prog Album of the Year 2013

The Raven That Refused To Sing (And Other Stories) is Steven Wilson's third solo album, released in February 2013. It's based on ghost stories written by Wilson himself, similar in style to those of 19th-century authors Charles Dickens and Edgar Allan Poe. The album's title evokes Poe's 1845 poem *The Raven*, in which the raven eerily cries 'Nevermore!' Wilson's stories are not investigations into the paranormal or the supernatural but are literary and existential investigations into the human condition. In an insightful interview with Anil Prasad of *Innerviews* in 2013, Wilson said, 'For me, ghost stories are like metaphors. They're symbols of regret and signify a human soul unprepared to depart because something is unfulfilled in the real world during one's lifetime.' As an atheist, Wilson believes you only have 'one shot' at life. To him, reaching the end of one's life, without being with the person you should have been with, without having the career you wanted, or without being creatively or emotionally fulfilled, is 'terribly sad.'

In February 2013, Wilson explained to Tom Davenport of *Ultimate-Guitar.com* that he found it hard to simply do nothing, to watch TV, or lie on a beach. He has a very strong work ethic, partly caused by the sense of guilt he feels when he's not working but also by his desire to 'leave something immortal.' In that sense, as he told Jeff Miers of *The Buffalo News* in April 2013, 'death can help to make meaning out of life', and that 'being creative is one of the ways we can make sense of the gift of life.'

Wilson recorded very detailed demos of the songs in advance, partly to save time in the studio but also to give his musicians a very clear idea of what he wanted. The music was so complicated that he had to play some of the parts at half speed on the demos. He told Prasad he had reached 'the highest level of complexity and difficulty I have ever attempted.' The virtuoso musicians he chose to realise his artistic vision had already toured with him in support of the previous album, *Grace For Drowning*: Nick Beggs (bass) and Guthrie Govan (guitar); Theo Travis (flute, saxophone and clarinet) and Adam Holzman (keyboards); and Marco Minnemann (drums). The band recorded around a song a day, although vocals were recorded separately – it wasn't until much later that Wilson gained the confidence to sing in front of a producer rather than on his own in his home studio.

The sound of the album evokes the classic prog rock sound of the 1970s, when Yes, King Crimson, Pink Floyd, Camel, Genesis, Jethro Tull and Emerson Lake & Palmer were arguably at the peak of their creativity. Prasad put it beautifully:

> It's an unabashed audio love letter to fans of the best of 1970s progressive rock. It captures the organic energy and borderless, long-form approach of the era and pairs it with Wilson's omnivorous musical psyche.

Wilson himself admitted to Davenport: 'I'm a great believer that records sounded best in the 1970s. I don't really like the sound of modern recordings, including most of my own.' But the album wasn't a mere pastiche of the earlier era. He wanted it to sound 'timeless' rather than 'retro for the sake of it.' In his 2022 book *Limited Edition Of One,* he admitted to being proud of the album, but also said he sometimes regretted making it, as it reinforced preconceptions about him and his relationship with traditional prog rock.

Wilson chose Alan Parsons to capture that classic sound. Parsons had engineered perhaps the best of the 1970s prog rock albums, Pink Floyd's *The Dark Side Of The Moon* (1973). After his success with Pink Floyd, he formed The Alan Parsons Project, releasing *Tales Of Mystery And Imagination* (1975) based on the works of Edgar Allan Poe, including a single *The Raven* (November 1975). Parsons told Prasad that what persuaded him to work as the engineer on the album was not only the fact that Wilson wanted a 1970s sound but also that Wilson told him the band was going to record live together in the studio, 'that's really what clinched it for me.' He was also impressed by the fact that the band were recording in EastWest Studios, Los Angeles, where there was a classic Neve mixing desk from the 1970s. Parsons was involved with another album recorded live in the studio, The Beatles' *Let It Be* (1970), at the same time as the film of the same name. Parsons can be seen in Peter Jackson's 2021 documentary *Get Back* about the making of the album.

With Parsons at the mixing desk, Wilson could act as musical director in the studio. He trusted Parsons to record the band all together. As Adam Holzman told Prasad, 'It's becoming a lost art. Most engineers record one instrument at a time.' In a fascinating series of YouTube videos, 'Steven Wilson In LA' (September and October 2012), the band can be seen setting up their gear and working on songs including 'Luminol', 'The Watchmaker' and 'The Holy Drinker'. Travis and Holzman play woodwind and keyboards in isolation booths in corners of the studio to stop their parts bleeding into the rest of the sound. The rest of the band – Wilson and Govan on guitar, Beggs on bass and Minnemann on drums – sit in a large live room, with relatively few microphones, placed at some distance from the drums and guitar amps. The result is a richly organic sound, far from the sterile cut-and-paste techniques that recording and mixing on a computer can sometimes encourage. In particular, Minnemann's spontaneous, enthusiastic and fiercely improvisational drumming comes across very clearly on the videos, as it does on the album itself.

The cover was designed by German artist and photographer Hajo Müller. He first worked with Wilson on Porcupine Tree's 2009 album *The Incident*. His distinctive, apparently scribbled drawings, often very dark in style, can also be seen on the compilation albums *Drive Home* and *Cover Version*. In March 2016, Müller told Sami Wakim of *Street Art United States* that he suggested the 'solitary moon' drawing for the cover, 'it's simple but clear, a good drawing, very emotional, something that represented the album perfectly.' The image also looks like a ghostly screaming face, evoking the ghost stories on which the album is based.

Like all of Wilson's solo albums to date, it was initially available in a limited edition box set. In a YouTube interview with *Metal Blast* in November 2013, Wilson was asked whether his music needed the extra media that comes with a deluxe box set to 'convey its message to the listener.' He replied, 'The music has to stand on its own anyway.' But he admitted that the music is 'enhanced by visual representations, particularly with this concept', referring to the fact that the ghost stories were available only in the deluxe edition. With both this album and *Hand. Cannot. Erase.*, there's additional visual material in the deluxe box set that deeply enhances the story and the overall concept. These enhanced editions are true works of art and can bring great pleasure to their owners. But this can cause difficulties for fans who can't afford the box sets, or only discover Wilson's music long after they have sold out. Copies do appear for sale online, sometimes at vastly inflated prices. Some are in the original shrink-wrap, which suggests that they have been bought as collectors' items, or perhaps even as investment opportunities. Wilson himself satirised this in the Limited Edition Box Set for *The Future Bites*. Those who opened the box were greeted with the sarcastic (but probably truthful) message, 'Congratulations. By opening this Limited Edition Box Set, you have succeeded in halving its value.'

In 2022, Wilson published his ghost stories 'Luminol' and 'The Raven That Refused To Sing' in the second volume of the Special Edition of his book *Limited Edition Of One*.

'Luminol' (12:10)
Luminol is a chemical used by crime scene investigators to detect the presence of blood invisible to the naked eye, but the title seems to bear no relation to the song. There's no blood in Wilson's ghost story, which can be found in the Deluxe Edition. Here's a summary:

> The town busker always stood in the same spot, whatever the weather, playing an old acoustic guitar. He never learned the songs properly and never seemed to improve. One winter, he collapsed and died on the spot where he always played. At the funeral, there were no friends or relatives, only a few people with nothing better to do. A week later, the busker was back at his regular spot, continuing to play despite his recent death.

Wilson told Joe Bosso of *Music Radar* in February 2013 that the story was inspired by 'a guy who plays in my local town', playing his acoustic guitar every day, never getting better 'no matter how much he plays.' This led Wilson to wonder what would happen if the busker sadly dropped dead on the street – would anyone notice? Then he thought the busker was 'so set in his routine that even death wouldn't stop him.' It's a clever conceit – as Wilson said, the idea is that 'somebody can be a ghost in life as well as in death.' Wilson returned to the idea on *Hand. Cannot. Erase.*, which is also based on a real person, Joyce Carol Vincent, who became so invisible that no-one noticed she had died until around three years later. The song itself doesn't refer to the busker's return after death. It opens with a reference to the passage of life, being born into 'a struggle', then ending up 'returning to dust'. There's no suggestion of an afterlife, even as a ghost. Instead, the busker's attempts to make something of his life as a musician are gently mocked: 'he strums the chords with less than grace.'

The song was premiered live on the second part of the tour to support *Grace For Drowning*, and the live version can be heard on *Get All You Deserve* (2012). Wilson told Bosso it was an experiment to see how it worked in front of a live audience. He concluded it 'all worked out very well.' On the live version, Niko Tsonev plays guitar, but was replaced in the studio by Guthrie Govan.

The track begins with a bassline played by Beggs, with a meaty tone sounding very much like Chris Squire of Yes. This was deliberate, as Parsons told Prasad in 2013, 'They said, 'Make it sound like Chris Squire." He achieved the distinctive, trebly sound by putting the bass through a Marshall guitar amp rather than recording directly into the mixing desk.

Keyboard player Holzman's deliciously dirty Fender Rhodes soon provides a further proggy delight. The sound is processed by a ring modulator, giving it a distorted tone; the effect is used to create the voices of the Daleks in *Doctor Who*. Holzman told Prasad he first used the effect on the live version of 'No Twilight Within The Courts Of The Sun' from *Insurgentes* (also on *Get All You Deserve*). Of all the solos on the album, the one on 'Luminol' was the only one that Holzman had to work out in advance rather than improvising during the recording session. He told Prasad that the song has 'an alternating 4/4 – 15/8 pattern, and the bassline was tricky to match harmonically.'

The song cements its prog credentials at around 6:30 with a brief burst of Mellotron that sounds very similar to Rick Wakeman's keyboards for Yes on 'Heart Of The Sunrise' from 1971's *Fragile* (at around 4:53). Wilson's remix of *Fragile* didn't come until 2015, but presumably he knew that album well before remixing it. The Mellotron on 'Luminol' is the original Mk II Mellotron used on King Crimson's classic prog rock album *In The Court Of The Crimson King* (1969).

Travis, who played extensively on the previous album, provides jazzy flute solos. Usually, Wilson allowed Travis to fill with a wind instrument of his choice, but on 'Luminol', he already knew he wanted him to play the flute. Travis told Prasad that Wilson would often simply say, 'Play wilder', 'Play sparsely', or 'Try some long notes'.

'Drive Home' (7:57)

'Drive Home' was voted number 91 in the 100 Greatest Prog Anthems of All Time in *Prog* in March 2017. At the time of writing, the song has had over 14 million plays on Spotify and nearly ten million views on YouTube, making it the most popular song of Wilson's solo career.

The story of this incredibly moving song is very simple. Wilson told Bosso that it's 'a sad, very beautiful song about loss.' The protagonist is driving his car when his wife or girlfriend inexplicably disappears from the passenger seat beside him. It transpires that he has completely erased the traumatic memory of a car accident in which she died. Years later, she returns as a ghost to remind him of 'what happened that night.' He can't understand where she has gone: 'A moment in time suspends/How could she leave?' She tries to persuade him to 'clear away/All the jetsam in your brain/And face the truth'. The story was Müller's idea, and in the Deluxe Edition, he illustrates it with a few compelling images. In March 2016, he told Wakim it was originally called 'The Story Of Charles And Lucy', based on a series of paintings he had done 14 years earlier. It was 'too long, so [Wilson] started with the song in about the middle of the original story.'

The videos for the title track and 'Drive Home' were created by Jess Cope, and both are different from the songs in fascinating ways. In a YouTube interview, 'The Making Of 'Drive Home'', in October 2013, Cope explained that Wilson is always happy for her to build on his characters, but in this case, the video adds additional depth to the story and to the emotional impact of the song.

Cope didn't want to repeat what she did for the title track, but to create something that was 'a little bit less supernatural or maybe a little bit more psychological' to represent the protagonist's repression of his traumatic memory. She created an 'ominous dark figure ... his unconscious self, stealing away all the mementoes that might remind him of his lost love.' We see this figure stealing the woman's hairbrush and throwing it into the water near the scene of the fatal accident.

The two-dimensional cut-out animation represents the past, his repressed memories, and the three-dimensional stop motion animation represents the present. In both cases, the (unnamed) Charles' head is made of newspaper – a papier-mâché orb with wire-rimmed metal glasses. Cope said that using the texture of newspaper was the cheapest way to make the two worlds the same, but somehow she gives expression to Charles' face. The result is profoundly moving, and we deeply empathise with him. In the video and also in one of Müller's images, Charles is seen writing letters on a typewriter. This isn't mentioned in the song, but according to Jess:

> Steven's original story was all about this man who is trapped in this world of letter writing to his lost love, but he has no address to send them to, and if you look in the house, there are just stacks and stacks of letters, so I think it just kind of tied in with that story.

In the video, Charles is in a wheelchair as he types the letters, whereas in Müller's original image, he's sitting in an armchair. It's unclear why there is a difference, although perhaps the implication in the video is that Charles has been injured in the car accident. He tries to drag Lucy out of the car, but tragically, he fails to do so as it bursts into flames.

Müller said Charles' house had to be created for the video 'because this was never shown in any of the illustrations'. This adds greater poignancy, as the house is very close to the scene of the accident. A great deal of the story in the video – including the accident itself – takes place on or near a lake with a small jetty, and at 4:20, Charles looks through his window and sees the lake. If the accident happened near his home, driving home means returning to the scene of his trauma rather than coming home to find sanctuary.

Wilson wrote this song and 'The Watchmaker' on an Ovation acoustic guitar that a fan gave him. He told James Rotondi of *PremierGuitar* in April 2013 he couldn't accept 'such a generous gift.' But his guitar tech, 'Tonto' Jhowry, said it was a lovely gift, so Wilson accepted it. Jhowry re-strung the guitar in Nashville tuning, using lighter strings (otherwise they would snap). This means tuning the bottom four strings (EADG) up an octave and leaving the top two strings (BE) as they are. Wilson told Rotondi that the tuning has 'that wonderful crystalline quality – I find it incredibly inspiring.'

After the opening guitar motif, Wilson's voice creeps in, heavily modulated, making it sound almost like an instrument. This is Charles' voice, which contrasts with the much more open-sounding vocals in the chorus, accompanied by lush orchestral strings, representing the ghostly but deeply compassionate voice of Lucy.

Govan's guitar solo, which starts at around 5:00 and lasts to the very end of the track, is simply astonishing. It's matched only by his solo on 'Regret #9' (*Hand. Cannot. Erase.*). Both are the perfect combination of emotion and virtuosity, starting with long, sustained notes which glide in (played here with an Ebow, a hand-held electronic bow) and moving to much faster virtuosic phrases. Basil Francis, in a typically fascinating and insightful roundtable review for *DPRP,* says that Govan's musicianship 'breaks new boundaries because no-one has ever made the humble guitar sing the way he does here.' Wilson told Bosso that Govan did four or five takes of the solo, all improvised and all completely different. Wilson chose an early take, 'It was so inspired and had such a beautiful sense of logic and storytelling to it. It's one take, unedited, and it's just unbelievably brilliant ... I was almost in tears.'

Remarkably, as Govan told Rotondi, the E string popped out of its saddle on the Fender Jazzmaster, due to some 'extravagant string bending'. He carried on playing, and the other members of the band declared it the best take despite the technical mishap.

'The Holy Drinker' (10:13)

The title of this song is an oxymoron, contrasting a holy man with an alcoholic. Wilson told Bosso he was thinking of hypocritical 'TV evangelist types', who are very happy to tell their audience 'That [they] have all these vices, and meanwhile they have plenty of their own.' The song's protagonist suffers a 'curse', the 'unquenchable thirst' of the alcoholic. The use of the archaic words 'constant serfage' to describe the protagonist's relationship with alcohol suggests that this will be a medieval story, perhaps a parable, although Wilson himself said that the song is meant to be 'tongue in cheek.'

It's possible the title was inspired by the short story *The Legend Of The Holy Drinker* (1939) by the Austrian writer Joseph Roth, made into a 1988 film by the Italian director Ermanno Olmi, starring Rutger Hauer. A homeless alcoholic is lent some money by a stranger on the understanding that he will repay it to the local church when he can afford to do so. He constantly fails to repay the money, buying alcohol instead. The central character is given the chance of redemption by his encounter with the stranger.

The song also features an encounter with a stranger, but there's no possibility of redemption – it ends in damnation. The protagonist meets the stranger in a bar and challenges him to a drinking competition. What he doesn't at first realise – but listeners do – is that the stranger is the Devil, who 'rises from right out of the earth'. As Wilson told Bosso, 'You can't beat the Devil at a drinking competition.' The irony is that the protagonist has been warning others about sin and the Devil.

Wilson's use of religious imagery is interesting, bearing in mind he isn't religious. The protagonist is 'in rapt communion with himself', which suggests his narcissism, but the word communion also refers to the Christian rite. The lines 'This coffin was made from a tree/Please hammer in a nail for me' can be read literally, but there is also a strong Christian resonance. The wooden cross on which Jesus was crucified is often referred to as a 'tree', and nails were hammered into his hands and feet. The imagery appears extensively in Western art, music and literature. An early and very striking example is the Old English poem 'The Dream Of The Rood', which describes the tree that is cut down to serve as the cross on which Jesus is crucified, sharing his pain as the nails are knocked in.

Although the story is meant to be humorous, Wilson himself admitted to Bosso, 'the music is quite dark.' He described the opening instrumental section as 'a pretty furious rush of energy', inspired by the Mahavishnu Orchestra. The band are in full jazz-rock flight before the vocals enter, an astounding group of musicians at the peak of their powers, including some astonishing drumming from Minnemann at about 2:00.

There's a lovely, restlessly shifting series of chord changes at 3:00. The pulsating bass, with keyboard and flute embellishments, in the instrumental break from 5:00 is a joy to hear. The band also allow themselves a couple of spectacularly proggy moments: there's a repeated, highly syncopated riff played in unison by guitar and bass at around 3:30; and around 6:15, there's a repeated sequence of rapid key changes that snake back around on themselves. Wilson told Bosso that Holzman's Minimoog solo at around 8:30 is 'very evil-sounding.'

The song is unusual in not following a rigid tempo. Most contemporary songs – and many orchestral film scores – are recorded to a rigid, metronomic beat or 'click track'. This makes them much easier to edit as all the instrumental parts 'snap' to a fixed grid. It also means that when a song is played live, extra pre-recorded backing tracks and videos can easily be synchronised. The downside is that a spontaneous, human feel where the tempo subtly varies can sometimes be lost. Wilson told Prasad that when legendary drummer Bill Bruford was playing with Yes or King Crimson, he was 'speeding up or slowing down all the time', or Billy Cobham playing with the Mahavishnu Orchestra, 'like a juggernaut heading towards a cliff edge.' Wilson applied that technique to 'The Holy Drinker' to create momentum.

Wilson also wanted to create a musical journey. There's a remarkable, haunting section from 6:50 when the instruments drop away and we hear the cry of wolves, contemplative vocals and a funereal drumbeat before the song gathers itself again for the final, terrifying onslaught. It's a superb example of the changes in dynamics that characterise Wilson's songwriting at its best.

Parsons gets his one and only instrumental credit, playing 'haw-haw guitar'. This refers to the effect created by plugging an electric guitar backwards into a wah-wah pedal (haw-haw is wah-wah backwards). The effect was used by

David Gilmour on 'Echoes' from Pink Floyd's 1971 album *Meddle* to create the seagull effects. Parsons uses it around 7:00 for the sound of howling wolves, and again very briefly at the end of the track.

'The Pin Drop' (5:03)

This song and the next are murder ballads. Wilson told Prasad that both songs 'feature quite violent murders', and that murder ballads are songs 'about death and people being haunted by the ghosts of their loved ones or people they murdered.' 'Unquiet Grave' (which he arranged on *Cover Version*) is a traditional murder ballad.

Like the next song, 'The Pin Drop' is a study of the breakdown of a relationship that was always no more than a marriage of convenience. In each song, one partner – in both cases the man – eventually murders the other over apparently trivial matters.

Wilson told Bosso that this song is 'quite macabre'. It's sung by the murdered wife (hence the high-pitched vocals at the start): 'She's dead, she's been thrown in the river by the husband, and she's floating down the river while singing this song – from beyond death, beyond the grave…' She describes herself carried away by a river that 'passes through bulrushes on to the sea … I didn't deserve this bitter end'. This gruesome image has echoes of the Greek myth of Orpheus and Eurydice, the subject of several paintings and operas. Orpheus goes into Hell to rescue his dead wife Eurydice. Hades, god of the underworld, says he will allow them to leave Hell provided neither of them looks back. As they leave, Orpheus glances briefly back at Eurydice, and she disappears. Orpheus is then brutally murdered and his body dismembered, leaving only his head, which floats down the river, singing. Müller's rather disturbing image in the Deluxe Edition of the wife's head floating down the river, singing, could easily be a picture of the head of Orpheus.

The title of the song plays on the idea of it being so quiet you can hear a pin drop. Wilson subtly adapts this to suggest that the 'tiniest thing', such as the sound of a pin dropping, is enough to trigger a violent rage in the husband, a measure of the fact that there's 'so much tension, so much unspoken resentment and hatred' in the relationship. This is the first time in his solo career that Wilson writes from a female perspective, as he did on the next album, *Hand. Cannot. Erase.*

The shortest song on the album, it acts as a bridge between two much longer songs. Although, as Wilson told Joe Basso, it's 'one of the simplest pieces on the record … it was also the hardest to get right.' Its simplicity meant that musical interest and variety had to be maintained by the way the song is 'layered and structured'. Later in his solo career, when he had the confidence to write even more straightforward pop songs on *To The Bone* and *The Future Bites,* it might have been simpler still.

The vocals at the start lie very high in Wilson's range, creating a sense of tension and feverish energy. He told Bosso that he 'opened his throat and sang in a less contained, less controlled way.' His role model was Nick Harper, son of the English singer Roy Harper.

After that, the voice is mixed with rich backing vocals, but the track remains anguished throughout, illustrating the chilling image, 'I cannot feel my arms and legs/I don't deserve this bitter end'. Wilson's vocals are mostly set back very far in the mix, almost buried by the maelstrom of instruments around him, suggesting the way the protagonist was suddenly ripped away from her husband and from life itself, 'drifting off without a kiss'.

Travis contributes a frenetic sax solo, and Minnemann's drumming and percussion are tumultuous throughout. Govan's brief guitar solo is a perfect mix of the angular and bluesy. Wilson told Bosso that he fed Govan's guitar through a Leslie cabinet: 'It's such a wonderfully rich sound.' The Leslie cabinet is made up of a loudspeaker in front of which a drum rotates, creating a varying tremolo effect according to the speed of rotation. It was originally used with the Hammond organ, but later was used by The Beatles to modify vocals, such as on 'Tomorrow Never Knows' (*Revolver*, 1966). At the very end of 'The Pin Drop', you can hear the sound of the rotating Leslie cabinet.

'The Watchmaker' (11:42)

This song features another violent murder. An old watchmaker murders his wife of 50 years. His sight is failing with age, and at first, the song appears to be a gentle ballad about someone whose profession is ending, partly because of his age but also perhaps because the job itself is dying out. But there is a subtle menace beneath the apparently elegiac tone. The poetic image of the cogs in the watches as they connect with each other contrasts with the 'curse' that time itself has left. And the smooth grace of the cogs as they connect together when they are mended contrasts with the marriage, which is beyond repair, beautifully summarised in the words: 'Fifty years of compromise/And ageing bodies shared'.

At this point, we don't know that the watchmaker has killed his wife – there is a 'shadow on the staircase/Of someone from before'. It becomes clear a couple of verses later that the watchmaker's wife is no longer here – presumably due to her death, although that isn't spelt out. The lines 'I never really loved you/But I'll miss you anyway' are sung very sweetly, with the sense of regret that permeates the album.

There's then a long instrumental passage before the protagonist returns to contemplate the fact that the relationship was 'just meant to be temporary/ while I waited for gold'. In the final section, we hear the ghostly voice of his wife, who comes back to the watchmaker. The image of the relationship as a broken watch mechanism is cleverly reversed: 'Cogs and levers mesh/We are bound in death'. He can't escape his wife – the metaphor is extended to show that even if he were to try to melt down the 'silver' of the watch, she will still remain inside him.

The images created by Müller for the Deluxe Edition make the story more explicit. There's a very macabre picture of the watchmaker standing above his dead wife, whose head we see below him under the floorboards. This image is accompanied by the words 'Eliza dear, you know there's something I should say/I never really loved you but I'll miss you anyway'. Over the page is a horrifying image of Eliza coming back to haunt him, with the words 'We are bound in death my dear' echoing those of the song.

Wilson told Prasad the idea of 'the partner under the floorboards' was partly inspired by Edgar Allan Poe's short story 'The Tell-Tale Heart' (1843), a masterpiece of narrative economy, showcasing the power of rhetorical features such as repetition. It's also a fascinating study of the voice of the unreliable narrator, a literary term that was coined over a century later by Wayne C. Booth in his 1961 book *The Rhetoric Of Fiction*. The device was used by Emily Brontë in her 1847 novel *Wuthering Heights*.

Poe's narrator immediately addresses the reader and denies the madness of his behaviour, 'Why will you say that I am mad? The disease had sharpened my senses – not destroyed – not dulled them'. The story describes the narrator's decision to kill an old man, despite the fact that – in contrast to the watchmaker – he 'loved the old man'. The narrator claims there will be no financial or other gain to be had by murdering him. Like the watchmaker, something about the physical presence of the victim is enough to prompt murder – in this case, the irritating 'Evil Eye' of the old man. Again, like the watchmaker, the story's protagonist buries his victim under the floorboards. He's so efficient in hiding the body that when the police come, after a neighbour reports the old man's scream, he calmly sits on the floorboards above his victim's body while he chats amiably to them. The police continue to smile while the protagonist is haunted by the sound of the dead man's heart beating. Only he can hear it, and it's left delightfully ambiguous as to whether his victim has come back to life to haunt him – like the watchmaker's wife – or whether his guilt and paranoia are causing auditory hallucinations. The story ends with the protagonist shouting, 'I admit the deed! – tear up the planks! – here, here! – It is the beating of his hideous heart!' – the 'tell-tale' heart of the title.

The song is episodic, with long instrumental passages reflecting the personalities of the watchmaker and his dead wife. In most of the song, we see things from the watchmaker's point of view. The opening features chiming chords played on 12-string guitars. Wilson told Bosso he was 'very much inspired by the way Genesis used acoustic guitars early in their career.' He was probably thinking of songs like 'Supper's Ready' (*Foxtrot*, 1972). On that album, 12-string guitars were played not only by Steve Hackett, but also by Mike Rutherford and Tony Banks. Wilson said the 'chiming quality' of the 12-string guitar was the initial inspiration.

The opening melody is very sweetly sung with close-mic'd, intimate vocals from Wilson, and backing vocals from Jakko Jakszyk, best known for working with King Crimson. From about 2:00, a long, jazzy instrumental section begins, similar in style to much of the previous album, *Grace For Drowning*. There's a lovely, repeated chord progression from 4:00 to 6:00, reminiscent of the fragile, melancholy beauty of parts of 'Shine On You Crazy Diamond' from Pink Floyd's 1975 album *Wish You Were Here*. At around 6:00, the track stops, and the next section begins with a delicate, undulating piano melody that gradually comes into focus. The vocals return, with the message that his wife was only 'meant to be temporary'. The gorgeous, wordless vocal section that follows creates tension between the music and the lyrics. The song is about a murderer, but the music belies that.

A new section at around 9:00 is marked by a bass solo, and at this point, the murdered wife appears. We hear her ghostly voice with its chilling message, 'We are bound in death'. The meshing of 'cogs and levers' is graphically described by the growling, grinding instruments. At 9:45, there's a very short burst of progressive metal guitar, a riff that could have come from the genre that mixes heavy-metal riffs with the complexity of prog rock, lasting only a few seconds. Roger Trenwith of *DPRP* thoughtfully highlights this little moment: 'You can all but imagine this strangely understated prog-metal riff winking at you as it slips by barely noticed.' Admitting it was probably idle speculation, he wondered at the time if this was 'a final goodbye to the world of Porcupine Tree', whose later albums often featured such riffs. The song climaxes with frenetic drumming, and a short Mellotron chord brings another epic to a close.

'The Raven That Refused To Sing' (7:57)

Voted number 40 in the 100 Greatest Prog Anthems of All Time in *Prog*, March 2017. In his book, *Limited Edition Of One* (2022), Wilson lists this song as one of his top five 'most depressing songs'. The track tells the story of an old man, Eliah, and his older sister, Lily, who died in childhood. The story was written by Wilson and Müller, and the text can only be found in the Deluxe Edition. Here's a summary:

> Eliah wakes up alone in the small, run-down house he has lived in for years. He forces himself out of bed and looks out of the window at the snow. He imagines he hears a girl weeping, and hums a nursery rhyme from his childhood to try to drown the sound. He shouts, 'Please stop it'. The sound stops, and his day begins.
>
> Eliah remembers when he was seven, finding a dead sparrow with his sister, Lily. She told him that snow would come that night and take the sparrow to a better place. Eliah relied completely on his sister to calm him and protect him. The snow came that night, and the sparrow vanished. The snow purified the earth, but later Eliah discovered it could reveal things that should be left hidden, and his childhood turned into a nightmare.

When Eliah was about nine, Lily became very ill. He looked after and prayed for her, but one night, as the snow began to fall, she died in his arms. His sister had left him alone on Earth, and after feeling despair, he felt nothing.

Eliah often struggles to sleep, wishing that Lily would come and take him to a better place. He wakes one night, and the hall door is open, even though he's sure he'd closed it. He sees a shadow coming towards him. He pulls the covers over his eyes and feels the weight of the shadow on him and smells decay. Lily comes to comfort him, and the shadow disappears.

Eliah wonders whether Lily and the shadow were just his imagination. He leaves the house and walks in the fresh snow until he sees a raven sitting on a fence. They stare at each other, but when Eliah gets closer, the bird flies away. As he walks home, he senses that the raven is watching him and feels they will meet again. He loses his way and sits on a fallen tree in the cold, wondering if he should just die here. He thinks his life is pointless; he could at least become a useful meal for the creatures in the forest. The raven flies at him, cawing, and he runs home. Later, he wakes up and realises that the angry raven in his dream had been telling him that his life serves no purpose.

Eliah doesn't dare leave the house after his encounter with the raven, but sees the bird regularly in his garden. Rather than malice in the raven's eyes, he can only see sadness. He thinks that the raven can bring him salvation, and resolves to catch the bird. He feeds the raven regularly, and they begin to build a relationship. In the meantime, he builds a cage.

Eliah sets up the cage with a trail of bait and waits. From his hiding place, he sees crows who are tempted by the bait and hopes they are a good omen. The raven appears and eats the bait. Looking directly at Eliah, he stops outside the cage. Eliah fears he's been found out, but the raven steps inside the cage to eat the final piece of food. Eliah traps the bird.

The trapped raven appears to accept his fate and feeds from Eliah's hand. Eliah tells the bird that he will look after him, but he can't leave. The raven seems to understand. Eliah asks the bird to sing for him, but the raven remains silent. He yearns for the raven to sing and to bring him comfort and protection, just as Lily had done when she sang for him.

In Eliah's dreams, the raven sings to him. It's the most beautiful sound he has ever heard. In his waking hours, he tries to get the raven to sing to him by humming Lily's song, but the raven ignores him.

The raven gets weaker and seems to be dying. Finally, Eliah loses patience with him and throws the cage across the room. He thinks he has killed his only friend. He goes outside as spring appears, but the warmth doesn't console him. On his return home, he sees the cage door is open. The raven looks reproachfully at Eliah and flies away.

Eliah has again lost everything that was dear to him. He lies down to die. He hears Lily's voice, saying she will never leave him again. He feels the beating of her wings. She sings to him, and he feels years of pain and suffering lifting from him. He cries as they are united again.

There's a fascinating comparison between the story and the lyrics of the song, which are inevitably much less detailed. The poetry of the song, compared with the prose of the short story, lies in the economy of expression, which hints at the full story. The poignant backstory of Eliah and his sister Lily is painted in the simplest of brushstrokes, 'Sister, I lost you/When you were still a child'. The raven sings to Eliah in his dreams, which is identified in the printed lyrics by the simple stage direction, 'the raven sings in a dream'. The rest of the lyrics express Eliah's fervent hope that the raven will sing to him, and that Lily will also sing to him. The raven and Lily become intertwined in the incredibly moving final verse, in which Eliah alternately pleads with the raven and Lily.

The video, superbly directed by Jess Cope, adds in some extra detail from the original story. It opens with Eliah, a wizened old man with a haunted look, walking in the woods, picking up firewood. In the story, Eliah hears the sound of a girl (Lily) weeping, and in the video, she appears as a vision. He meets the raven, who sings to him, and again later in his garden. In the short story and the video, a shadow appears. It seems to kill Lily in the video, whereas in the story, Lily comforts Eliah as the shadow disappears. In both the story and the video, Eliah entices the raven into a cage and traps it. The raven refuses to sing, and Eliah angrily picks up and throws the cage, apparently killing the raven. The raven then escapes.

The above analysis demonstrates how a simple but compelling narrative can be equally effective in different media. The video and music together are available not only on the *Drive Home* EP but also on YouTube. It's significant that Wilson uses the video as a backdrop when playing the song live, as can be seen on the *Home Invasion* video released in 2018, suggesting that, in his mind, the two versions of the song go together. But the song stands on its own as well.

For a more detailed analysis of the way the short story, the song lyrics, the music and the video interact to create a unique piece of art, it's well worth reading the chapter 'Interpreting Transmedia And Multimodal Narratives' by Professor Lori Burns of the University of Ottawa in *The Routledge Companion To Popular Music Analysis: Expanding Approaches* (2020). As Burns says, 'taken as individual elements ... important details of Wilson's narrative development remain elusive, and we are unable to form a complete reading of the narrative', with the emphasis on the word *complete*. As she points out, 'without the illustrated story ... there is much about Eliah's experience – even his name – that we do not know and understand.'

The song begins with ambiguous string chords, clusters of notes that create a sense of unease. Wilson used a similar technique at the start of the song 'Drag Ropes' from his 2012 Storm Corrosion collaboration with Mikael

Åkerfeldt. The feeling of ambiguity is present throughout the song, particularly in the repeated opening piano riff. Three simple chords lead to a fourth chord of C minor. When the pattern is repeated, the fourth chord is now C major (the E flat is converted to an E natural). In emotional terms, this creates a constant pivoting between a sad (minor key) chord and a happy (major key) mood, which makes the listener feel unsettled. The constant repetition of the chord sequence eventually gives it a monumental quality, a sense of inevitability, as the pattern is quickly etched on the listener's brain, and we come to expect those chords each time they come round.

The first three chords are played in 3/4 time (waltz time) with one beat per chord, and the fourth (a long held note of four beats) is played in 4/4 time (the time signature for nearly all pop and rock songs). Alternating two bars in different time signatures effectively creates (as Burns points out) a phrase which is in 7/4 (one bar of three and a second bar of four). This gives the track a restless quality.

The raven's voice is synthesised. Parsons' song 'The Raven' from *Tales Of Mystery And Imagination* also features a synthesised voice, Parsons' own voice put through a vocoder. Burns describes the effect in Wilson's song: 'the entry in the vocoder … marks a technological intervention: the eerie melody suggests the warbling and trilling of a bird, but with an otherworldly quality.' Burns perceptively points out that in the second half of the song, Wilson's voice is doubled an octave below by his voice put through a vocoder: 'the voice is masked and doubled by the vocoder, creating a link to the earlier vocoder presentation and extending the voice in pitch and timbral space.' Although Burns doesn't directly suggest this, it could be argued that this represents Eliah's hope that the raven will sing with him. At the end of the track, Wilson's vocals gradually become swamped by the instruments, as if completely overcome by emotion, or as Burns puts it, 'ultimately the voice is overtaken sonically by the accumulation of instrumental timbres, the level of intensity and the use of space.'

The song feels very personal, as reflected in the heartbreaking, anguished cries of the word 'please' from around 3:00. The emotional power of the track is such that Davenport asked Wilson how much it was based on personal experience. Wilson admitted it was difficult to answer. He doesn't have a sister, and has never lost one, 'but at the same time, a lot of the sentiment, a lot of the feeling is absolutely from me.' He said the song is about someone who has never been able to bond with any other human being since he lost his sister: 'His life has just been one long feeling of loneliness and loss.' He felt that almost everyone who watched the video or listened to the song would understand those feelings, even though their personal story was very different: 'It's not autobiographical, but a lot of the emotional resonance comes from the feelings that I have experienced in my life.' Although he didn't mention the loss of his own father in this interview, he dedicated his previous album, *Grace For Drowning*, to him, and his 2022 book, *Limited*

Edition Of One. He also said in an interview with Jerry Ewing of *Prog* in February 2015, talking about *Hand. Cannot. Erase.*, 'My father had just passed away when I wrote *The Raven*, so it stands to reason that I was in a much darker place then.'

Guille Palladino, in his review for *DPRP*, says the ending of the song is happy, as the raven, the old man's sister, will sing for him and 'she will take him with her to the next life.' Palladino says:

> For me, this is a great metaphorical story, and perhaps the only one on the record with a happy ending, because sometimes we all have a need to stay with our beloved ones, and for one reason or another, this is not possible, but in this case, death is the solution.

It's a fascinating and compelling suggestion, but it's at odds with Wilson's own interpretation. Wilson told Bosso that 'in his ignorance, he decides that if he can get the raven to sing to him, it will be the final proof that this is, in fact, his sister, who has come back to take him with her to the next life.' The key words here are '*in his ignorance*', suggesting that the old man is deluded. This doesn't mean, of course, that Palladino is wrong – all great art is open to multiple, equally valid interpretations. The music itself could provide the clue here. The piece appears to have reached a triumphant conclusion with a final cadence at around 7:25, which could suggest a happy ending. But this is overshadowed by a ghostly coda, with the same unsettling string chords we heard at the start, followed by a simple but devastating restatement of the main chorus theme ('sing to me, raven/Lily I miss you/her so much'), implying that the raven doesn't sing and Eliah isn't reunited in death with Lily. Where Palladino is undoubtedly correct is when he says that the song is 'the highlight of the album and an excellent closing theme, the perfect crescendo song.' However you interpret it, this song is one of the best that Wilson has written.

Hand. Cannot. Erase. (2015)

Personnel:
Steven Wilson: lead vocals, Mellotron, keyboards, guitars, bass, banjo, hammered dulcimer, programming, shaker, effects
Guthrie Govan: guitar, lead guitar
Nick Beggs: bass, Chapman Stick, backing vocals
Adam Holzman: piano, Hammond organ, celesta, Fender Rhodes, Wurlitzer, Moog Voyager synthesiser
Marco Minnemann: drums
Dave Gregory: guitars
Chad Wackerman: drums on 'Happy Returns'
Ninet Tayeb: vocals on 'Routine' and 'Ancestral'
Theo Travis: flute and baritone saxophone on 'Ancestral'
Katherine Begley: spoken word on 'Perfect Life' (incorrectly credited to Katherine Jenkins)
Leo Blair: solo vocal on 'Routine'
Schola Cantorum of the Cardinal Vaughan Memorial School: choir
London Session Orchestra: strings
Producer: Steven Wilson
Recorded at Air Studios, London (September 2014), No Man's Land, Hemel Hempstead, EastWest Studios, California (drums on 'Happy Returns'), Angel Studios, London (strings)
Release date: February 2015
Highest chart placings: UK: 13, US: 39
Running time: 65:44
Current edition: Kscope

Hand. Cannot. Erase. is Steven Wilson's fourth studio album. The concept is based on the life of Joyce Carol Vincent and the grim story of her death. Joyce was found in her London flat in January 2006. She had been dead for nearly three years. Her body was only discovered when bailiffs broke in to recover rent arrears. The post was piled up behind the front door, there was washing in the sink and the TV was still on. Joyce was surrounded by unopened Christmas presents. Her body was so badly decomposed that she had to be identified from dental records. The inquest was unable to establish the cause of death.

Joyce's neighbours didn't notice her disappearance or the smell coming from her flat. The story was reported by Jerome Starkey in *The Sun* in April 2006. One of the neighbours said, 'People keep themselves to themselves in this block.' Another added, 'In other countries, people know all their neighbours, but not here.'

Wilson learned about Joyce's story from the 2011 drama-documentary *Dreams Of A Life* directed by Carol Morley. In an article for *The Observer* in October 2011, she said she was haunted by the image of 'the television flickering over her decomposing body.' This led her to ask, 'In a city such as London, home to eight million people, how could someone's absence go unnoticed for so long?'

Talking in January 2015 to Phil Simon of *HuffPost*, Wilson said, 'Most people would assume that [Joyce] was a lonely little old lady.' In fact, she was only 38 when she died. She had a good job, working for the accountants Ernst & Young. She had ambitions of being a singer. She became friendly with the American singer Judy Cheeks and met Stevie Wonder, Jimmy Cliff, Gil Scott-Heron and Isaac Hayes.

Wilson told Simon that he'd first become aware of Joyce when the story broke in 2006, but had learned far more from Morley's film. The documentary haunted him, and as he told Jordan Zivitz of the *Montreal Gazette* in June 2015, 'I don't mean to sound pretentious, but sometimes it's almost like the subject matter chooses you.'

On a Twitter Listening Party hosted by Tim Burgess of The Charlatans on 21 April 2021, Wilson said, 'It's important to say that the album is not the story of Joyce; it only takes the circumstances of her death as a starting point to create a narrative about a completely fictional character.' He created the album's protagonist – she's never named – as a means of expressing and embodying his thoughts about 'life in the 21st century, the internet, social networking … loss and nostalgia for childhood and isolation.'

Wilson naturally found Joyce's story shocking and sad, but he told Zivitz she was 'actually not a terribly tragic figure, although she died in very tragic circumstances.' In his view, 'her isolation was her choice.' He could see the attraction of withdrawal from modern life in the city: 'It's almost analogous to the whole idea of being a songwriter … you're making observations, kind of unobserved yourself.' But her story does say something damning about the way we can ignore our fellow human beings in a big city. Wilson told Simon that he understood how this could have happened. He himself had lived in London for 20 years, and 'I never knew my next-door neighbours.'

Moving back to his hometown of Hemel Hempstead made Wilson appreciate how isolated it's possible to become in a huge metropolis like London. He told *Face Culture* on YouTube in 2015 that Hemel Hempstead had a much greater sense of community: 'I know all of the people on my street, I know the name of my postman, I know the name of the local policeman.'

Returning to his childhood hometown reawakened strong memories: 'Every street corner, every street, every park, every tree has a kind of nostalgic memory for me.' Nostalgia became one of the themes of the album and a strong part of the protagonist's character.

Wilson told *Face Culture* that his protagonist was based very closely on his own life: 'Almost everything that happens to my character, and some of the dreams and some of the thoughts she has, most of them are mine.' He told Zivitz that, in contrast to some of his previous concept albums, 'it feels very personal and it feels very real.' In his 2022 book, *Limited Edition Of One*,

Wilson tells tragic stories from his childhood. His Uncle Leonard starved himself to death after being made redundant, and his body wasn't found for several days. And a close family friend, 'Auntie' Audrey, killed herself after her children got married and her husband left her.

It's interesting that, as a man well into his 40s, Wilson chose to write from the point of view of a young woman who is 30 years old when we first meet her in her blog and 36 at the end of the blog. In March 2015, he told Mike Mettler of *Digital Trends* that on every record, he gives himself a new challenge, in this case, 'the story being written from a female perspective.' Parts of *The Raven* were written from a woman's point of view, but this was the first time he had based the whole concept of an album on a female perspective. Ironically, as he told Stephen Humphries of *Under The Radar* in March 2015, writing from this perspective actually allowed him to be 'more honest' in revealing more of himself. He also wrote a diary of the protagonist as a girl. He told *Face Culture* that to 'write from the perspective of a 13-year-old teenage girl was even more of a challenge.'

The Deluxe Edition of the album was created by Wilson himself, Lasse Hoile and the graphic designer and artist Carl Glover, with artwork by German illustrator Hajo Müller. Wilson said on the Twitter Listening Party that it was 'definitely the most ambitious one [we] had created at that point, and it took a lot of discussion and planning. I spent a long time writing the diary of the main character.' He also created an incredibly detailed blog for her. He told Zivitz that 'a lot of that stuff I wrote in the blog was stuff pretty much from my own life and my own thoughts.'

In photos taken for the Deluxe Edition book, the blog and videos used in live shows, the protagonist is played by the Polish model Carrie Grr (Karolina Grzybowska). She told Sebastian Gabryel of *Głos Wielkopolski* in April 2016 that she loved Hoile's work on the video for 'Harmony Korine' (*Insurgentes*) and approached him to see if he needed a model. He immediately agreed to use her – there was no casting, so she 'appeared in the project like a 'Deus ex Machina'.'

Hoile spent two weeks in Poland with Carrie in August 2014. They were joined in Poznań by local photographer Krzysztof Czechowski, who appeared as a model in one of the photographs. He and Carrie shot all the concert films over a period of several months. They were joined by the Lebanese photographer and filmmaker Youssef Nassar, who also shot the videos for 'Perfect Life' and 'Happy Returns'.

The video for the title track was shot in Hoile's hometown of Aarhus, Denmark. Wilson said on Twitter, 'In my mind, I had an idea of how my character would look, and she wasn't really it, but, of course, now it's hard for me to think of the character as anyone but Carrie. I didn't actually meet her until a show in Poland on the first leg of the *HCE* tour.'

Wilson said on Twitter, 'I wanted the [Deluxe Edition] book to have various loose inserts, evidence of a life ... the big task designing all the elements was mostly taken on by Carl [Glover].' In the *Face Culture* interview, he said the plan was to reproduce the items so that they 'look authentic', to give a real insight into the protagonist's life – important for a character who has largely given up communicating with the outside world. The book provides unique and realistic artefacts, beautifully recreated, including a sketchbook, newspaper cuttings, a postcard, a birth certificate, a letter, a handwritten mixtape cover (the playlist can be found on Spotify by searching *Dream Kitchen Mixtape*) and the diary.

From the blog dated 9 March 2011, we learn that the protagonist collects stories of missing women, 'those who simply vanished one day without any warning.' She muses that the women may have chosen to disappear, just as she herself chooses to do. Their stories are therefore not about loss and tragedy but about 'escape and rebirth', women liberated by the chance to start again.

All the stories are convincingly told in fictional newspaper reports. Florence Duncan disappeared in March 1911 at the age of 23. Teresa Cavanagh, a 'quiet and reserved' 32-year-old secretary, went missing from Bristol in November 1999. Jane Rimer, a student at Rochester University, went missing on 16 April 2006, having been 'more distant and distracted than normal.' Other women, Madeleine Hearne and Lena Springer, are referred to in the tracks 'Routine' and 'Ancestral', respectively, although not named on the album.

Perhaps the most striking of the other missing women is Sian Preston, who disappeared in June 2002. Her story is similar to that of Joyce Carol Vincent, except that when the bailiffs broke into her flat after 'several final demands', she had disappeared. There may be poignant echoes of Wilson's own career. Preston always wanted to be a professional singer, and 'worked really hard to make it happen, but she got so disillusioned after she moved to London.' The parallel with Wilson's life is not exact, of course, but it did take 30 years from the formation of Porcupine Tree in 1987 to the release of *To The Bone* in 2017 for one of his albums to reach the top ten in the UK album charts. So when Wilson writes of Preston that she 'found it much harder than she expected to get noticed', there's an emotional truth here. And Wilson told Dave Simpson of *The Guardian* in August 2017 that the album was 'really about me, being invisible in plain sight – a metaphor for my career.'

Humphries, in a typically perceptive interview, suggests that the album ends on 'a hopeful note', in contrast to Joyce's tragic ending – the protagonist is trying to reconnect with her loved ones, specifically her brother and his family, in the penultimate song 'Happy Returns'. Wilson agreed that the end of the album is upbeat, but stressed that it's 'definitely ambiguous.' It's unclear what happens to her character at the end of the story. He told Humphries that there's a 'little frisson of sci-fi possibility.' This is made much more explicit in her blog, in which she talks about, in Wilson's words, 'visitors in the night and people talking to her about some other place.' The visitors are a major presence in the blog. They talk to her about her childhood, they prowl around her flat, they leave her a book called *Keys Of Skeleton*. She feels uneasy when she doesn't hear from them for a while, and she sees their lights in the sky.

But it's never clear whether the visitors are real. In a blog dated 5 June 2011, she sees 'something else in the sky' but reassures herself that 'I must be dreaming again.' In the entry dated 2 December 2014, the question is posed, 'Why do I stay?', presumably referring to her staying on earth or remaining alive. 'I think the visitors ask me this, or maybe I just ask myself in my head.' And in the entry dated 8 September 2009, she talks about her artwork, some of which appears in the book, as a way of 'decoding the world I saw.' The text in some of the artwork refers to 'visitors', and she says, 'I really wasn't sure myself if what I was painting and drawing was real or in my head.' When people asked where the strange images in her art came from, she 'knew instinctively it was not something I should talk about.'

The visitors could be hallucinations brought on by a mental health condition, or they could be aliens who abduct her at the end of the album. The track 'Ancestral' refers to 'those who live alone' in the city – like the protagonist – who 'see things that aren't there when they close their eyes.'

For listeners who enjoy conspiracy theories and puzzles, there are further riches. In May 2018, Wilson told Argentine journalist Fabrizio Pedrotti that 'Home Invasion' and 'Ancestral' contain spoken numbers that are 'part of a puzzle ... with which you can discover what happens to the character, if you have the special edition. But I think nobody has solved it yet because it's very hidden.' There are online communities dedicated to solving the puzzle. On the Quadraphonicquad website in May 2018, 'César' revealed that the numbers – in the Deluxe Edition book itself, and also on the cover of the *Key Of Skeleton* insert – are geographical locations. On Twitter, Ava asked for 'any words of advice for the 75 dedicated fans in the *HCE* deluxe edition puzzle-solving server?' Wilson cryptically replied, 'It's all about the map references!'

The title of the album is also mysterious. Wilson told Phil Simon he could have called it *The Loneliness Of Living In The City*, but that would have been too limiting. He told *Face Culture* that he was unhappy about having to give it a title at all, so he compromised with an ambiguous title: 'It's a little bit enigmatic even with the way it's punctuated', referring to the strange use of full stops. All he would reveal was that the keyword is 'erase', saying that the protagonist 'chooses to erase herself in a sense.' Her blog at handcannoterase.com has also now disappeared – the artefacts and images in the Deluxe Edition book still preserve parts of her life. (A further irony is that the Deluxe Edition itself has also disappeared from view. As a limited edition, it's now been deleted from the catalogue, although second-hand copies are still available to buy at the time of writing.)

On the original album, there are 11 tracks, but on streaming services, three tracks are segued with the next one ('First Regret/Three Years Older'; 'Home Invasion/Regret #9'; 'Happy Returns/Ascendant Here On...') to make a total of eight.

'First Regret' (2:01)

This track opens with the sound of children playing, instantly evoking nostalgia for childhood. Wilson said on Twitter, 'The piano was made to sound broken and wobbly, like the music was a memory of something gone, rusted and decayed.' It's a type of 'lo-fi' sound used by Wilson to create nostalgia for the wobbly-sounding, often sonically poor cassette tapes of his childhood. Karel Witte, on a *DPRP* roundtable review in February 2015, said this nostalgic sound is 'blatantly borrowed from electronic music pioneers Boards of Canada.' In June 2013, on Twitter, Wilson himself said that the group's latest release, *Tomorrow's Harvest*, was 'album of the year (so far) for me, what a beautiful record...' The heavily filtered rhythmic sound at the start of opening track 'Gemini' can be heard at the start of 'First Regret'. The piano motif reappears at the end of the album, opening the track 'Happy Returns'.

Although it's a short, simple track, Adam Holzman plays a variety of keyboards – piano, celeste and Hammond B3 organ, and Guthrie Govan a smattering of guitar. The sound of rain that appears at around 0:30 evokes a rainy school playground but also gives the track a grainy feel, adding to the lo-fi sound.

'Three Years Older' (10:18)

Wilson said on Twitter that the track 'sets up this character, with scenes from her childhood.' She's viewed by an objective narrator who, in the verses, addresses her as 'you'. In the chorus, this shifts to a more empathetic viewpoint: 'I can feel you more than you really know'.

The title could refer to a moment of the protagonist's childhood frozen in time, 'You're three years older/and you'll always be now'. It could also refer to the close friend the protagonist describes in 'Perfect Life', who was three years older than her.

But there's also a darker interpretation: Joyce Carol Vincent was found nearly three years after she died, as if she had been frozen in time. The line 'shame on you for getting older every day' implies that the protagonist should leave this world, perhaps through death: 'the world will slip away'.

The childhood scenes aren't as nostalgic as in other Wilson songs. The protagonist crosses the schoolyard (perhaps a nod to Wilson's 2008 No-Man album with Tim Bowness, *Schoolyard Ghosts*) with 'head held down', suggesting shyness, anxiety, or even depression. There is some hope, though. The cloud breaks as the protagonist walks the streets. This is also a metaphor – rather than the sun appearing from behind the clouds, 'a hundred futures' come cascading out. The infinite future possibilities that childhood promises are contemplated here: 'it's complicated'.

Sadly, as the song reveals later, the world closes in, and all the possibilities are narrowed down to a life in which the protagonist cuts herself off, and now: 'it's not complicated'. She's found 'a simple life with no-one to share'. Her tragic existence is revealed towards the end of the song – she's like one of the lonely, desperate characters she sees from out of her apartment window.

Wilson said on Twitter, 'The music for this developed during sessions for my previous album, *The Raven That Refused To Sing*. It has the more traditional prog rock aspect of that album. Maybe it's a bit old-fashioned in that respect, but it does open things up in epic style.' Various critics have pointed out that this track and the title track have strong similarities to Rush and Manic Street Preachers.

Someone from @burningshednews (Burning Shed) tweeted Wilson to say that the acoustic guitar riff at the start reminded them of The Who. Wilson replied, 'Haha, yes okay, the patch in my live pedal board for this part was called 'Townshend', so guilty there!'

Wilson plays bass guitar on the song. He admitted that the bass sound is heavily influenced by Chris Squire of Yes, possibly because he had been working on Yes remixes. As he told Humphries, 'I play the bass like a guitar player does ... I have a guitarist's mind and a guitarist's sensibility.' He said his approach to bass playing is 'more of a lead approach … [Squire] started out as a lead guitarist, too.' Wilson also plays acoustic guitar on the song, with other guitar parts played by Guthrie Govan and Dave Gregory.

The vocals are emotionally raw, presumably due to Wilson's habit of recording his vocals at home in his studio at the moment of inspiration when writing the song and not re-recording them later to polish them. The vocals are enriched by lush backing vocals. There's a lovely piano solo from Holzman, played with an exquisitely delicate touch. The song ends with a deliciously proggy display of virtuosity. There's a dirty, funky, jazzy Hammond solo followed by a raucously wailing guitar. Finally, there's a restatement of the main instrumental, and a gently satisfying cadence on guitar.

'Hand Cannot Erase' (4:17)

Wilson said on Twitter that the title track is about 'being in a relationship and kidding yourself that it's working when it clearly isn't.' The lyrics can be found on a postcard in the Deluxe Box Set addressed to 'B.F.' (presumably 'Best Friend'). The address is 210 Maydew House, Abbeyfield Road, London SE16 2DP. Maydew House was a 26-storey 1960s tower block. When Wilson wrote the album, the tower had 168 flats, meaning that flat 210 didn't exist. There were plans to add five floors, but the building was demolished in the summer of 2025.

In the blog dated 1 January 2015, there's a reference to a letter the protagonist finds floating in the wind, 'a love letter, possibly unrequited. Either it was never sent, or the recipient simply threw it away.' This is followed by the words 'Hand cannot erase this love'. The upbeat chorus of the song, which uses these exact words, is poignant as it's not so much a celebration of love as a mourning for its loss, a sarcastic refrain.

In the blog dated 19 December 2009, the protagonist admits, 'Okay, so there was one person I got close to.' There's a picture of her with a photographer she met in her second year of college. She liked the idea of being his muse, like 'Lee Miller to his Man Ray' (Miller was a photographer and Ray was an artist who worked in the Surrealist and Dadaist styles). But she felt she was always playing a role, 'a dream of a life' (the title of the documentary about Joyce Carol Vincent). All the time she was with her (unnamed) boyfriend, she was 'counting the seconds' until she could 'be on my own again', and she eventually ended the relationship, erasing the love that 'hand cannot erase', using the classic lover's excuse: 'It's not you.'

Although the song is clearly seen from her point of view, Wilson sings the lead vocal (although backing vocals are provided by Ninet Tayeb). To the casual listener, the song could therefore be an epic ballad about the power of love, but the context makes it something much more interesting. The constantly shifting points of view on the album make it a much deeper and enigmatic experience.

The uneasy nature of the song is emphasised by the unusual and rather awkward rhythm. Most pop and rock songs are written in four beats per bar. This song is written in nine beats per bar. Wilson has mentioned on various occasions that when his father built him a step-sequencer for programming synth patterns, it worked in groups of nine rather than the conventional eight or four, perhaps instilling a prog rhythm sensibility into the teenage musician.

The Canadian cellist Raphael Weinroth-Browne, who describes himself on his website as having 'a passion for progressive metal', has recorded a beautiful, emotive cover of the song arranged for nine cellos.

Hoile's video was used as the live video for the song before being released online. Shot in black and white, it features the protagonist and her lover, mostly in happy times but with hints of the breakup to come.

'Perfect Life' (4:46)

Wilson said on Twitter that 'The words were originally written as a short story with more lines. I hired a voice actress to read it, but when she did, I realised it would make the song too long, so I cut it back to the key lines…' The story is about a childhood friend that the protagonist had for a short time: 'When I was 13, I had a sister for six months.' Although the word 'sister' appears to be metaphorical in the context of the song, meaning a close friend or even soulmate, her blog reveals that her sister was briefly adopted. But the most important aspect of the relationship is the profound influence that the 16-year-old had on her younger sister, introducing her to music, books, clothes and her 'first cigarette'.

The song includes some very precise memories from Wilson's own childhood. The voiceover refers to the 13-year-old protagonist sometimes going with her sister to 'Blackbirds Moor to watch the barges on Grand Union Canal in the twilight'. In the *Face Culture* interview, Wilson said, 'It's a very vivid but real image from my childhood.' In February 2015, Jerry Ewing of *Prog* described walking along the Canal back to the railway station with Wilson before Wilson cheerfully announced, 'I'm off to visit my mum', with whom he was going to spend Christmas. As Ewing said, 'It somehow all seems fitting.'

There's been some confusion about the actress who recorded the voiceover. She was originally credited as 'Katherine Jenkins', perhaps referring to the Welsh singer, but it is, in fact, Katherine Begley. Wilson told Lilen Pautasso of *Reverb Magazine* in August 2016 that he approached an agency but couldn't find exactly the right voice. Begley's voice was 'different to what I imagined, but I grew to love it.' Her languid approach perfectly matches the nostalgia and regret of much of the album and the cool electronic atmosphere of this track. As the album is seen from a female perspective, Wilson felt not only should he have a female singer on some tracks, but 'I also wanted to have, literally, a female voice on the record.'

The blog dated 12 August 2009 includes the complete voiceover, but also some additional information about the story. The song doesn't explain why the album's protagonist had a sister for only six months. The blog reveals that her parents adopted her sister, but 'later that year, my parents separated and my sister was rehoused with a family in Dollis Hill.' It's easy to see why Wilson deleted this reference from the album, as it detracts from the poetic image of the girls being close and then passing into distant memory without any explanation. The poetry of the image is heightened by the reference to the Canal itself, 'water has no memory', which conjures up the philosophical concept of not being able to step into the same river twice as it's constantly moving and evolving. It's an idea that also appears in the Porcupine Tree song 'Oceans Have No Memory' (*Recordings*, 2001).

In the diary, the protagonist describes a visit to London with her adopted sister (referred to as 'J'), where she is excited to find out how far the Canal reaches: 'Didn't know that the Grand Union runs through Camden, too!' Although 'J' drops out of the album after this song, she continues to be an important part of the blog. In the entry dated 17 December 2014, the protagonist writes, 'I know you are reading this, J.' On 23 January 2015, she says the two have made contact again, linking her comment to the mix tape that appears in the Deluxe Edition of the album, 'You and me, J, only hearing the music, speaking to me again now through the tape hiss of time.' This suggests a spiritual rather than a literal connection. The next entry, dated 27 January, sees the protagonist and her 13-year-old self discussing the fact that their sister is 'waiting for us'. This may refer to the fact that J is with the visitors if indeed they do exist. The mystery is increased by the fact that these entries only appeared on the online blog, which is no longer available, and not in the printed version of the blog in the Deluxe Edition of the album.

Wilson said on Twitter that the song, the last one he wrote for the album, marked a change of musical direction, 'Although the band I had at the time was capable of playing very 'muso' and complicated music, I was definitely

Above: Steven Wilson live at the Blue Balls Festival, Lucerne, Switzerland, in 2016. (*Alamy*)

Left: *Insurgentes*, Wilson's first solo album, released in 2008 while he was still active with Porcupine Tree. (*Kscope*)

Right: 'Postcard', released as a single from *Grace For Drowning* in 2011. (*Kscope/ Transmission*)

Right: *Grace For Drowning*, Wilson's second solo album, released in 2011, marked a jazzier direction in his solo career. (*Kscope/ Transmission*)

Left: *The Raven That Refused To Sing (And Other Stories)*, Wilson's third solo album, released in 2013, is a tribute to classic 1970s progressive rock. (*Kscope/ Transmission*)

Above: Wilson performing live at the Shepherd's Bush Empire, London, in 2011. (*Getty Images*)

Below: Wilson and band live in Milan, Italy, on 10 May 2012. (*Alamy*)

Above: Nick Beggs, Steven Wilson, Guthrie Govan and Marco Minnemann during the recording sessions for *The Raven That Refused To Sing* at EastWest Studios, Los Angeles. (*Lasse Hoile*)
Below: Guthrie Govan playing the guitar solo from 'Regret #9' during the recording sessions for *Hand. Cannot. Erase.* at Air Studios, London, in September 2014. (*Lasse Hoile*)

Left: *Hand. Cannot. Erase.*, Wilson's fourth solo album, released in 2015, features a female protagonist who isolates herself from the modern world. (*Kscope/ Transmission*)

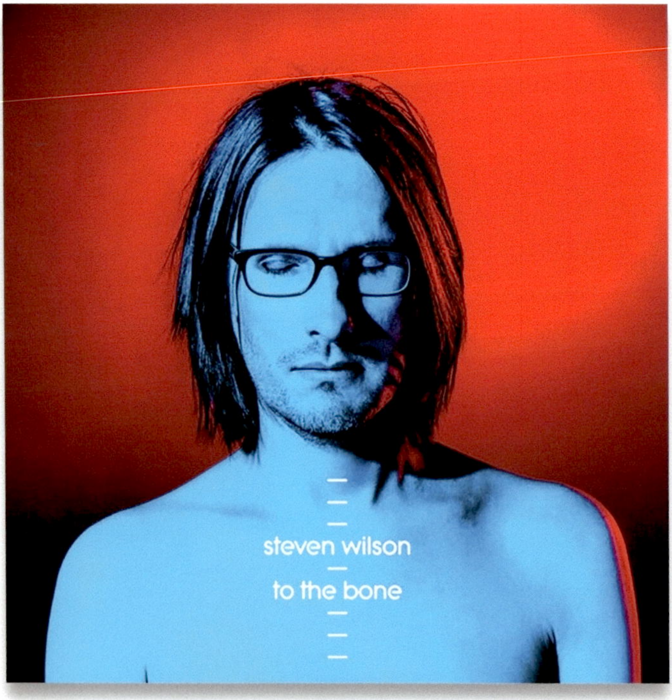

Right: *To The Bone,* Wilson's fifth solo album, released in 2017, was influenced by the sophisticated pop of Peter Gabriel, Kate Bush, Talk Talk and Tears for Fears. (*Caroline International*)

Above: Wilson in his home studio, 'No Man's Land', in Hemel Hempstead, in February 2015. (*Will Ireland/Total Guitar Magazine/Future via Getty Images*)

Right: A concert poster for Wilson's gigs at the Royal Albert Hall, London, in support of *Hand. Cannot. Erase.*

Above and below: Nick Beggs on Chapman stick and Craig Blundell on drums during the *Ask Me Nicely – The Making Of To The Bone* documentary, filmed in 2016/17. (*Lasse Hoile*)

Above and below: Wilson with singer Ninet Tayeb and keyboard player Adam Holzman during *The Making Of To The Bone* documentary. (*Lasse Hoile*)

Left: *Unreleased Electronic Music*, released in 2004. Wilson wrote, 'My real love might just be electronic music.' (*Tonefloat/ Headphone Dust*)

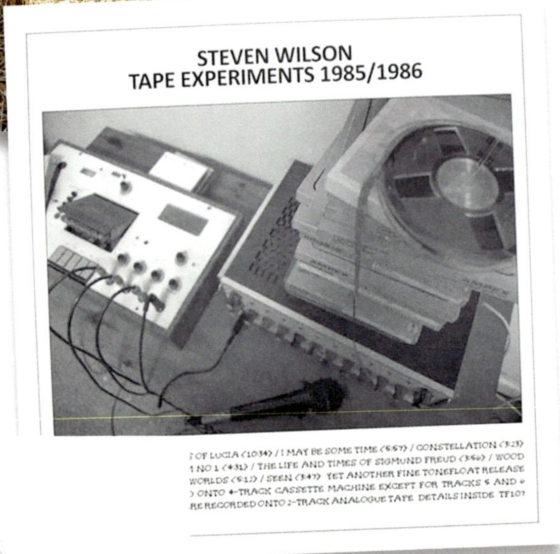

Right: *Tape Experiments 1985/86*, released in September 2010. Wilson wrote: 'Various attempts to make academic avant-garde electronic music ... of historical interest only.' (*Tonefloat/Headphone Dust*)

Left: *The Cover Version* compilation album, released in 2014, consists of six *Cover Version* singles released in 2003-2010. Wilson described the singles as 'the first steps in my career as a solo artist.' (*Kscope*)

Right: *Transience*, released in 2015, showcases 'songs recorded between 2003-2015: an introduction to the more accessible side of Steven Wilson.' (*Kscope*)

Left: *STVN WLSN – NSRGNTS RMXS*, released in 2009, features remixes of Wilson's first solo album, *Insurgentes*. The title leaves out all the vowels. (*Kscope*)

Right: *Drive Home*, released in 2013, was described by Wilson as 'a video EP ... essentially a single from *The Raven That Refused To Sing*, but so much more!' (*Kscope*)

Above: A promo shot for *To The Bone*. (*Lasse Hoile*)

Below: Steven Wilson in the Royal Albert Hall, London.

Above: From the *Home Invasion* live album: Wilson and Bollywood dancers perform 'Permanating'.

Above: Wilson and his rhythm section performing 'Ancestral' on the *To The Bone* tour.

Above: Singer Ninet Tayeb performing 'Pariah' on the *To The Bone* tour.

Left: *4½*, the EP released in January 2016, with songs from *The Raven That Refused To Sing* and *Hand. Cannot. Erase.* sessions. (*Kscope/Transmission*)

Right: *Insurgentes*, a road trip documentary about the making of Wilson's first album, was released in 2010. (*Kscope*)

Left: *Last Day Of June* (Original Game Soundtrack), released in August 2017, features music based on songs from Wilson's solo albums and his Bass Communion project. (*SW Records/Caroline Distribution/ Music on Vinyl*)

Right: *Catalogue / Preserve / Amass* – Wilson's first solo live album. The title comes from the lyrics of 'Index', from *Grace For Drowning*. (*Headphone Dust/ Kscope*)

Left: *Get All You Deserve*, recorded live at Teatro Metropolitan, Mexico City, on 13 April 2012, was released in September 2012. (*Kscope/ Transmission Records*)

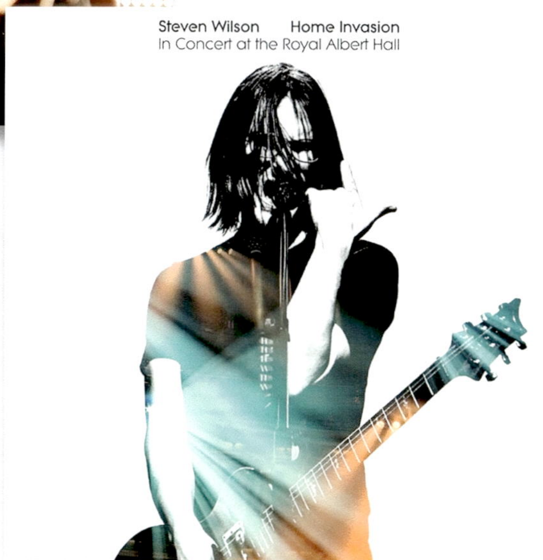

Right: *Home Invasion: In Concert At The Royal Albert Hall*, recorded during the *To The Bone* tour on 29 March 2018, was released in November 2018. (*Eagle Vision/Universal Music Group*)

Above: Wilson's book, *Limited Edition Of One: How To Succeed In The Music Industry Without Being Part Of The Mainstream*. (*Constable*)

tiring a bit of that ... My interest was also moving away from guitars and towards electronic sound.'

The song is one of several on the album to feature the Ghostwriter VI (Virtual Instrument), a sample library and production toolkit created for the Eastwest company by Wilson and producer Doug Rogers. According to the Eastwest website, it can be used to create 'dramatic and terrifying soundscapes ... the professional composer's single most powerful tool for creating horror and suspense on demand.' It's a fascinating insight into Wilson's production techniques, with a wide palette, including a sweet Mellotron and edgy, distorted sounds that could be used in a horror film soundtrack or a song in the style of Nine Inch Nails.

Minnemann's drums are heavily treated to give an industrial, electronic sound. At just over 2:00, the drums become more aggressively industrial, suggesting the emotional wrench caused by the two girls being forced apart. Wilson's voice, choirboy-like as befits the innocence of childhood, describes the 'perfect life' the two briefly shared, an elegy for a long-lost relationship. Beggs adds subtle falsetto backing vocals with a slightly ethereal quality to emphasise the perfection, matched by the sparkling keyboards. Beggs also provides a gentle solo on Chapman stick from around 4:00. The vocals become more anthemic and layered as the song reaches an epic conclusion before coming to an abrupt stop, like the relationship itself.

The video was made by Youssef Nassar. Wilson said on Twitter, 'I asked him to watch Peter Weir's haunting film *Picnic At Hanging Rock* to get an idea of the kind of atmosphere I wanted.'

'Routine' (8:58)

'Routine' was voted number 44 in the 100 Greatest Prog Anthems of All Time in *Prog*, March 2017. It's possibly the saddest, most moving song Wilson has written. In his book, *Limited Edition Of One* (2022), he lists it as one of his top five 'most depressing songs'. On Twitter, he said, 'Sometimes I joke on stage that even if I'm famous for writing miserable songs, even I am stunned sometimes by how truly depressing and sad some of them are!' On the *Insurgentes* DVD, he makes some very revealing comments about why so many of his songs are sad. He explains that he lives his life, as many people do, on a fairly even keel emotionally, but has occasional 'crystalline moments of melancholy' which provide inspiration in his songwriting: 'Music that is sad, melancholic, depressing is in a kind of perverse way more uplifting'. In contrast, he finds happy music 'extremely depressing, mostly ... music that has no spirituality behind it, just sort of mindless party music. Although he doesn't describe sad music as cathartic – many listeners will find that a song like 'Routine' has exactly that effect – he does say such music makes us feel 'like you're not alone.'

The depth of compassion that Wilson shows for parents who have lost children is evident in 'Routine'. It's worth pointing out that Wilson has not lost any children himself, and he now has two stepchildren following his marriage in 2019. He has very happily and openly shared images of 'The Wilson family' on social media. On Instagram in December 2021, he posted cheery Christmas photos of his new family, prompting postfernandobop to comment, 'Stop being happy and enjoying company! We need you depressed to make the best possible music! (Just joking).'

So how did Wilson get the idea for the song? He told Greg Prato of Songfacts in February 2016 that he was taking his daily walk around town and 'the idea just popped in my head.' He decided to write a song about 'the mechanical process of everyday existence being used somehow to block out reality.' As the poet T.S. Eliot said in 'Burnt Norton' (*Four Quartets*, 1941), 'Human kind/cannot bear very much reality'. Wilson said that becoming absorbed by routine, 'the daily grind', can sometimes be a way of avoiding the bigger existential questions, and that the idea probably came from 'a very personal perspective.' He created a tragic story of a woman who has lost her family and is going through a 'very extreme psychotic denial, in that she uses her daily work routine ... to basically deny the reality that is obvious to the outside perspective.' It's the mundane details of her everyday domestic routine that make the song so heart-wrenching and poignant. She describes the children's clothes as 'such tiny things that still smell of them', suggesting that her bereavement is still recent and raw, but also that there is a degree of obsession in her constantly cleaning and tidying the empty house. It's matched in emotional depth by a song Wilson wrote for Porcupine Tree, 'Heartattack In A Layby' (*In Absentia,* 2002), where the precise, mundane details of the layby where the protagonist goes (unknown to him) to die heighten the terrible reality of the tragedy: 'I pull off the road/East of Baldock and Ashford'.

The song's chorus and some of the later verses are sung by the Israeli singer Ninet Tayeb. In the chorus, she describes how 'routine keeps me in line', preventing her from feeling emotion about the tragedy. So it's shocking, and incredibly moving, when she lets out a scream at 7:20. The scream was improvised and surprised Wilson. On Twitter, he said he hadn't asked her to do it, 'but it made the hairs on the back of my neck stand up when she did, a magical moment.'

Wilson told Mettler that he auditioned three or four singers and chose Tayeb because she managed to '*elevate* the music beyond what I expected.' Humphries was surprised Wilson had chosen a singer who had been the winner of the Israeli version of *Pop Idol,* bearing in mind Wilson's 'disdain' for such shows, which he was later to express in the song 'Move Like A Fever'. It's a fair point, but Wilson's reply was equally telling: 'She started out as a pop artist ... but she reinvented herself as an almost kind of PJ Harvey-type alternative figure. A very brave thing to do.'

What's not immediately clear is how this song relates to the protagonist's story, except in the sense that it's about a woman who is completely isolated, having withdrawn from the world due to the tragic loss of her family. The narrative comes into much sharper focus in two newspaper articles from the Deluxe Edition. There's a loose newspaper cutting dated 17 September 1993, headed 'A Stolen Family'. The article describes a tragic primary school shooting in which Madeline Hearne lost her family when her husband and sons were murdered by 'unemployed taxi driver Keith Campbell', along with 21 other children and seven more adults. At the time of the massacre, Madeline was at home doing routine domestic chores. After going to the school where she learned of the deaths, she 'went home and carried on my routine of making the beds, laying the table and cleaning the house as if nothing had happened.'

A tragic story, but what really interests the album's protagonist is what happened next, after the song is finished. The second article, dated 19 November 1993, reveals, 'Stolen Family Mother Missing.' Thus, Hearne becomes one of the missing women whose stories the album's protagonist collects. This is the only time we gain a detailed insight into a missing woman's story and her reason for disappearing. It's a clever and very effective device, allowing Wilson to introduce another female character and a very powerful song without breaking the basic narrative concept of the album.

As Wilson said on Twitter, the structure of the song reflects three different stages of grief: 'denial, anger and then ... a kind of acceptance.' The song ends on a lyrical, poetic note of nostalgia and hope:

The most beautiful morning forever
Like the ones far off, far off away,
With the hum of the bees in the jasmine sway

The song's final lines elegantly and poignantly address the dilemma faced by anyone who has lost a loved one, the desire to remember them but also come to terms with their death: 'Don't ever let go/Try to let go'.

The song begins with Holzman's elegantly simple piano chords. There's a brief pause as we hear the sound of the sea, which the bereft mother's house overlooks. Wilson's vocals strengthen in character and resolve in the second verse, and Tayeb's chorus part is low in her register, showing her determination to carry on with her household routines. Above her floats an ethereal boys' choir, suggesting the character's true emotional state.

A robust celeste part played by Holzman reflects the character concentrating on her busy routines until the song drops away at around 3:00, revealing the depth of her grief. The music creeps back in with acoustic guitars and soft keyboard sounds until Govan plays a gentle Floydian guitar solo that keeps the emotion at a low level.

Tayeb then takes over the vocals in the verse, urging herself to 'keep cleaning, keep ironing' and 'cooking their meals', even though, tragically, there is no-one left to cook for. Delicate solo piano is subsumed by crashing, emotional chords on guitar and keyboards. The chorus returns, with Tayeb singing an octave higher than at the start, desperately trying to persuade herself that she is still coping. A very brief distorted guitar riff is topped by Tayeb's utterly devastating scream of pain. The song ends with tranquil, chorused guitar and Wilson's sweet vocals joined by Tayeb and the heavenly boys' choir. A beautiful end to one of the best songs Wilson has ever written.

Anne-Claire Rallo, in a fascinating and beautifully written article published in 2017, 'The Routine of Denial: Steven Wilson's 'Routine': A Sartrean Journey into Existentialism' in *Collecting Space. Essays On The Work Of Steven Wilson* (Anesthetize Productions, 2017)', describes an 'existential journey' through the song:

> We are invited to contemplate our own choices, confront our bad faith, and, ultimately, discover the authentic path to freedom, thereby echoing Sartre's enduring question: 'What is it to be truly free?'
>
> Rallo describes the protagonist's denial of the fact that her family is dead in Sartrean terms: 'anguish' (the anxiety that freedom brings) and 'bad faith' (self-deception, denial of one's own freedom of choice). She says that the protagonist, by interacting with objects that signify 'a deep connection to departed loved ones', blurs the lines between objects and human existence, an important distinction made by Sartre. The protagonist's existential dilemma is marked by her 'escape from her authentic nature' into grief and loneliness.
>
> Rallo describes the state of 'nothingness' that the protagonist must achieve to attain true freedom. She must avoid her existence being determined by past actions, reach a state of self-awareness, and embrace the future. She must accept the absurdity of existence rather than 'taking refuge in an illusory routine.' As set out above, the end of the song reveals hope for the protagonist. In Sartrean terms, this means accepting the absurdity of existence and embracing freedom.
>
> There is no need to know the philosophy of Sartre to understand the song, but Rallo does explain why the song has such a profound emotional effect on the listener, stating that Wilson's art 'always engages us on terrain conducive to the elevation of the soul without being influenced by a desire to please that would strip his message of its authenticity.

The video, which perfectly matches the emotions of the song, was made by Jess Cope. On Twitter, Wilson said it took her months to make, and she 'really went through an emotional rollercoaster doing it.' The stop-motion animation, with beautifully detailed and realistic artefacts, like the children's clothes and toys, heightens the emotion, making it almost unbearable to watch. At first, it seems to be the story of a house-proud woman obsessively cleaning and tidying, but her eyes are red with tears. The revelation of her devastating tragedy is foreshadowed by her cooking a meal and setting the table for four, but eating on her own. Then her emotions break through as she smashes a plate and starts to mess up the immaculate house. The heartbreaking newspaper headline is then revealed: 'Father and two sons killed in school shooting'. She's seen from behind, screaming at the sky. But the video ends, like the song, with a moment of hope. She stares out to sea, as she does at the start of the video, but this time her face is serene.

'Home Invasion' (6:24)

This song provides the title of Wilson's second solo live album, *Home Invasion: In Concert At The Royal Albert Hall* (2018). Those who buy or stream it will allow the concert to invade their homes in the way that a criminal would. In the song itself, the 'invasion' refers to downloads from the internet.

On Twitter, Wilson described this as a 'funky dirty Fender Rhodes song', similar to 'The Holy Drinker' from *The Raven That Refused To Sing*. He said, 'I always have early Roxy Music in my head when I do those kinds of things.'

Wilson described the song to Phil Simon as a kind of musical journey: 'There's a jazz section [1.00 – 3:05], there's a funky section [3:05 – 4:07] and then there's like a spacey section [4:07 – 4.30].' Before the 'jazz section', there's a short instrumental intro in a fierce prog-metal style, similar to many of Tool's complex rhythmic riffs, or the closing section of 'Deliverance', the title track of Opeth's 2002 album. He said 'those kinds of songs are the hardest ones to put together ... you're trying to find the one way that makes the most logical sense...' It's something that Wilson has successfully battled with many times as a songwriter.

The song expresses one of Wilson's major concerns about 21st-century society: the effect of the internet and, in particular, social media, a theme to which he returned in more detail on *The Future Bites*. He told Simon that social media can become 'quite antisocial' in that it allows us to create a façade: 'Social networking makes it easier to disconnect.' This applies very clearly to the album's protagonist, who hides behind her blog, having withdrawn from the world.

The verses of the song refer to the dangerous side of the internet, which apparently allows the download of anything we want: 'Download the life you wish you had'. This is the voice of the cynical narrator, commenting on the protagonist's withdrawal from life into a virtual world where she can 'download sex and download god'.

The hard-driven funk of the verses contrasts with the spacey chorus, which shows the central character's point of view. The warm vocals and rich backing vocals poignantly express how isolated she has become: 'another day on earth has passed me by'. She's lost faith in the world outside, and the stars are like an awning 'in the wreckage of the night'. (This phrase is used in the blog dated 4 January 2015.) The night is described in a similar way in the previous song 'Routine': 'the dark comes to bruise the sky'. In the video for that song, the protagonist's house is completely isolated, and the central character in 'Home Invasion' is completely withdrawn, too, even though she lives in a big city; the parallel between the two young women is as clear as it is chilling.

'Regret #9' (5:00)

Wilson said on Twitter, 'As you can tell from the title, this is another one originally from the 'My Book of Regrets' project', the original album concept that was later abandoned. Wilson has said very little about the project: it's unclear whether there were any other 'Regrets' in the series. The album opens with 'First Regret'. The song 'My Book Of Regrets' was recorded during the *Hand. Cannot. Erase.* sessions and was released on the *4½* EP. That song seems to have been written from the perspective of the album's protagonist: her blog entry dated 12 December 2014 is titled 'My Book Of Regrets', and the chorus of the song includes those words:

All of this can be read
In my book of regrets

'Regret #9' is an instrumental that started life as 'a chord sequence I had that went around and around; I liked it but didn't know what to do with it.' It was only when Holzman added a Moog solo, and Govan added a guitar solo, that 'it suddenly sounded tremendous.' There's a YouTube video of Govan playing the solo at Air Studios in London. The intense concentration can be seen on Govan's face as he plays. When he completes the solo, he appears to breathe a sigh of relief or exhaustion, as if he's pleased to have got through it. It's a charmingly modest reaction to a superb, life-affirming solo performed in one take, a perfect mix of virtuosity and emotion.

The song ends with the sound of children playing that opened the album, another regret from the original concept, and contemplative piano chords.

'Transience' (2:43)

This song begins with an image of a child travelling on a train. This relates to Wilson's childhood nostalgia for trains, mentioned in various Porcupine Tree songs, including the gorgeous ballad 'Trains' (*In Absentia*, 2002). He grew up near a railway station and fell asleep each night to the sound of trains.

Although the song appears to be written from an objective narrator's point of view, referring to the protagonist as 'her', the viewpoint is the protagonist's own. In the blog dated 24 September 2011, she describes taking a train journey to the seaside in Wales, when she was four or five years old, at a time when she felt 'completely happy'. This was partly because she was passing through beautiful countryside, but also because she had her mother all to herself and her 'mother was happy that day', implying that she wasn't always happy.

She describes her happiest moments as being 'somewhere between departure and arrival', like the writer Robert Louis Stevenson's aphorism 'to travel hopefully is a better thing than to arrive.' In the song, the child in the train is described as 'Tristessa', an Italian girl's name derived from the Portuguese word 'tristeza' or 'sadness'. It's also the name of a 1990 single by The Smashing Pumpkins, who in turn took the name from a 1960 novella by Jack Kerouac, described on the cover as a 'novel about a morphine-racked prostitute'. But it's unclear whether the name is used here to express a deeper meaning. Perhaps it foreshadows the sadness that the protagonist suffers later in life. In a blog dated 10 January 2009, the protagonist notes that 'My mother is Italian by birth', so perhaps her mother chose an Italian name for her as a term of endearment.

What is striking is that despite learning a great deal about her through her blog, her artwork and the photos of her, we never find out the real name of the protagonist. The blog dated 10 January 2009 also includes the only words of advice her father ever gave her, 'that I had the whole of my life to get things right, and if things didn't make sense now, then don't worry, be patient. 'It's only the start."' These words form the chorus of the song.

This is the only song on the album on which Wilson plays and sings everything himself. He said on Twitter that it reminded him of 'Lips Of Ashes' (*In Absentia,* 2002); 'like that one, it's pretty much a solo performance.' The track contrasts acoustic guitars and folky, multi-tracked vocals that create a sense of nostalgia for childhood with a deep, ominous synth, suggesting that even in childhood, the protagonist had a darker side. There's a strong sonic and emotional link to the Pink Floyd song 'Goodbye Blue Sky' (*The Wall,* 1979). Although Wilson has sometimes been irritated by the Pink Floyd comparisons, he was happy to acknowledge the debt to *The Wall* here, as 'that album is so ingrained in my DNA even if I haven't heard it for maybe 20 years by now.'

'Ancestral' (13:30)

Voted number 58 in the 100 Greatest Prog Anthems of All Time in *Prog*, March 2017. The song is a mix of points of view. The verses reflect the view of an objective narrator, and the chorus seems to be the protagonist's own childhood memories. The first line of the song is ambiguous: 'Reason never seems to come to guilty men'. It's unclear whether it's aimed at the protagonist or is perhaps a more general indictment of humankind.

The second line of the song echoes the blog dated 4 March 2011: 'Sometimes things that mean so much at the time mean nothing in the end', referring to her brief but remarkably close relationship with her adopted sister and the fact that they never tried to find each other after they were forced apart.

The song seems to refer to the visitors and the women who have disappeared. The line 'Come back if you want to' appears to be quoting the line from the protagonist's penultimate blog: 'You can come back if you want to but no one ever does.' The protagonist's diary refers to an uncanny encounter with a girl of her age who turns to her and says the same line. Her response in the blog – but crucially not on the album – is 'I told them I'm ready, it's time to leave now.'

Of the women who disappeared, only Lena Springer returned, 78 years after disappearing without a trace, only to be killed immediately in a road traffic accident. According to the blog dated 28 March 2013, she died in 1954 at the age of 28, 104 years after her birth in 1876. This proves to the protagonist that some people do return: 'The visitors told me no one ever comes back, but what about Lena Springer?, I ask them.'

The chorus, seen from the protagonist's point of view, evokes childhood nostalgia. In a few short lines, an evocative image is created of summer holidays out on a bike, and a mother calling a child back home. It's so vivid that it seems to have come from Wilson's own childhood. The duet between Wilson and Tayeb almost suggests a shared memory: 'A bicycle/A garden wall/A mother's call/A love is born'. But the memory is marred by the final line, as sleet falls on the protagonist – 'and after all the sleet that falls on me' – so that she becomes one of the 'other fuckers in the rain' from 'Three Years Older'.

Wilson said on Twitter that the song is perhaps his favourite of all the long-form songs he's written, 'with a structure which feels like it's forever building towards something ... Even when you think it can't go any higher, it does.' It begins with a languorous, spacey trip-hop feel, sounding, as Karel Witte of *DPRP* in February 2015 put it, like 'Massive Attack meets Peter Gabriel', with hammered dulcimer played by Wilson himself and improvised jazzy flute flourishes from Travis. In the verses, Wilson's voice sounds remote and heavily compressed, whereas in the childhood memories of the chorus, his voice is much more intimate. The song builds to an epic guitar solo from Govan and virtuosic drumming from Minnemann. After some wordless vocalising, Tayeb sings the next chorus.

The second part of the song features a long instrumental section. From around 7:00, there's a hint of a heavy metal riff, coming into bloom at around 9:30. Although such riffs were such a feature on later Porcupine Tree albums, on his previous solo albums, Wilson had ditched that style completely. Humphries pointedly asked Wilson, "Ancestral' features some very heavy metal riffing. Are you a little less bored with it now?' Wilson replied, 'Metal is part of my musical vocabulary, but I don't think it would ever come back to the forefront.' He admitted that there are some 'quite heavy riffs' on this track and also to a lesser extent on 'Home Invasion', but also said the album includes electronics and the 'almost pop sensibility' of some tracks. And just when heavy metal seems to have established itself, music in the style of a film noir soundtrack appears with swirling flute. Witte described this as a 'labyrinth-like instrumental that's part King Crimson, part Meshuggah, part Mastodon and part Rush.' Heavy metal and film noir, then, join forces until just before 12:00, when a massive heavy metal riff appears. Wilson said on Twitter, 'The end of the song is not at a set tempo; it gets faster and faster, so even when you think it's settled at one tempo, it's actually still getting imperceptibly faster.' The song breathlessly rushes towards an exhilarating end until it finally expires, leaving a single solo guitar flailing around until it, too, gives up with a half-hearted strummed chord. A stunning ending to an amazing song.

'Happy Returns' (6:00)

In his book, *Limited Edition Of One* (2022), Steven Wilson lists this as one of his top five 'most depressing songs I have ever written', along with 'Routine'. As Wilson says, 'the whole album is generally pretty sad.'

The song is a letter the protagonist wrote to her brother, dated 22 December 2014, a physical copy of which can be found in the Deluxe Edition book, handwritten in blue ink on lined paper. In a blog dated the day before, she describes her relationship with him: 'I barely know my brother. I know he has a wife and two children, but I have no idea if he's happy or what is important to him.' Poignantly, she refers to the annual Christmas card she has just received from him and the invitation to visit that she knows she won't take up, 'for some reason, this time, it made me cry.' Perhaps this is because she now realises she will never see him again.

The song contains another train reference, although this time it's a simile for the passing of time rather than a childhood memory: 'The years just pass like trains'. On Twitter, David Cowie said, 'trains again!', to which Wilson replied, 'Yeah, the consistent motif in all lyrics across my career, I think.'

As mentioned in the introduction to this chapter, the end of the album is ambiguous. The letter and the song both end with the words, 'I'm feeling kind of drowsy now/So I'll finish this tomorrow'. This could be a note of hope, a suggestion that her life will continue the next day. Her words, 'I bet you thought that I was dead but I'm still here', contrast with Joyce Carol Vincent's tragic death. But on Twitter, Wilson said, 'Just like Joyce wrapping Christmas presents on the evening she died, things are left unfinished.'

So what happens next? In contrast with the words in the letter, in her final blog dated 28 February 2015, her last words are, 'I told them I'm ready, it's time to leave now.' Presumably, 'they' are the visitors, and she is leaving with them. The photos in the blog show strange lights in the sky, like those from an alien spacecraft. As Wilson said cryptically on Twitter, 'You can make up your own mind where the character goes.'

The track starts with a rumble of thunder, taking us back to the rain we hear at the very start of the album. The sound effects cleverly morph into a rhythmic motif leading into the return of the piano motif from the opening track 'First Regret'. The return of this theme makes the title 'Happy Returns' seem ironic, as it's returning in unhappy circumstances now.

Wilson's wordless vocalising at the start is haunting. Although the song is seen entirely from the protagonist's point of view – it's her letter – Wilson sings the words rather than using a female vocalist. The song begins with a simple, singer-songwriter feel, which matches the thoughtful approach of the letter. Wilson sings like a contemporary folk singer, his voice close-mic'd and honest, with more wordless vocalising at the end of the vocal section, 'doo doo doo...' The song becomes subtly epic, as instruments surround Wilson's voice, ending with a lovely but relatively subdued guitar solo from Govan. The contrast between the relatively epic instrumentation and the raw solo voice continues the feeling of ambiguity; are we witnessing the tragic ending of a human story, or a new beginning? The song ends with an unfinished feel, like the letter itself.

The video shows the protagonist reviewing her life as she writes the letter. She looks back at old photos, and there are some brief images from the earlier part of her life with her sister, taken from the 'Perfect Life' video, and even a couple of glimpses of a man who may be her brother.

'Ascendant Here On...' (1:54)

On Twitter, Wilson said "Ascendant Here On...' is almost an anagram of Hand Cannot Erase.' He's right – there's a missing letter 'A', but the rest of the letters are all used. It's strange to end the album with an instrumental, but as Wilson said, 'It's a reprise of the theme from 'Happy Returns' arranged for piano and the boy choristers.' The title of this instrumental seems to refer to the protagonist ascending into another dimension, or it could be a metaphor for a new, happier state (death?) into which she is passing. Cleverly, Wilson doesn't divide his listeners. Those who like stories of aliens can follow that story, and those who prefer poetic metaphors will be satisfied. Some may enjoy the ambiguity and hold both options in their mind at the same time.

To The Bone (2017)

Personnel:
Steven Wilson: vocals, guitars, bass, keyboards, Mellotron
Jeremy Stacey: drums
Craig Blundell: drums
Pete Eckford: percussion
Mark Feltham: harmonica
Adam Holzman: piano, Hammond organ, Clavinet, Wurlitzer piano, Solina strings, Fender Rhodes
Dave Kollar: guitars, guitar solo on 'Detonation'
Robin Mullarkey: bass
Nick Beggs: bass
Ninet Tayeb: vocals on 'Pariah' and 'Blank Tapes', backing vocals
Sophie Hunger: vocals on 'Song Of I'
Dave Kilminster: backing vocals
Paul Draper: Oberheim Sequencer
Jasmine Walkes: voice on 'To The Bone'
Paul Stacey: guitar solo on 'Refuge'
Synergy Vocals: choir on 'Song Of Unborn'
Producer: Steven Wilson
Mixed by Steven Wilson (except Cenzo Townshend, 'Permanating', and Paul Walton, 'To The Bone')
Co-producer: Paul Stacey
Recorded at No Man's Land, Hemel Hempstead, November 2015 and August 2016, Strangeways, London, December 2016 – February 2017, Angel Studios, London (strings)
Mastered by Tim Young
Release date: August 2017
Highest chart placings: UK: 3, US: 58
Running time: 59:46
Record label: Caroline International
Chosen as best progressive rock and metal album of 2017 by *PopMatters*

To The Bone is Steven Wilson's fifth solo album. Fans may be aware of the controversy on its release due to the apparent change of musical direction from the prog of *Hand. Cannot. Erase.* to the pop of the new album. *Prog* magazine put him on the cover in August 2017, posing the question, 'Has he ditched prog for pop?' On the bottom corner, a small disclaimer reassured readers, 'no he hasn't.' In a passionate plea to prog fans, Wilson spoke to Christina Pritchett of *World Prog-Nation* in August 2017:

> There is no sense at all that on this record I have sacrificed any of my sense of ambition, and the songs are just as sophisticated, just as layered and, in many respects, just as ambitious as any of my records have been.

So I hope that the progressive rock community will approach it with an open mind.

Although the new album marked a new direction, Wilson told Brice Ezell of *PopMatters* in August 2017 that he had always written pop songs: 'Every album has had at least a couple of direct, melodically focused pop songs on its track list.' But he admitted to Pritchett that if people saw him as 'someone that makes these very dark, intense conceptual rock records, then probably this is not the record for them.'

On his website, Wilson said he was influenced by the 'hugely ambitious progressive pop records' of Peter Gabriel, Kate Bush, Talk Talk and Tears for Fears. He'd been remixing Tears for Fears' albums *The Seeds Of Love* (1989) and *Songs From The Big Chair* (1985), and that rekindled his love of those artists.

Critics were divided, as shown by two reviews in August 2017. Philip Wilding of *Prog* said, 'It is a preposterously good mix of prog tropes ... and a clear-headed ear for melody and arrangement [that is] arguably his best and most complete solo album yet.' But Benjamin Bland of *Drowned In Sound* said, 'It works neither as a prog record nor as a pop record, and it certainly doesn't combine the two notions in a way that is anything to get excited about … it's just stylistically indecisive.'

Most of Wilson's previous albums had a very strong concept, which is part of what defines them as progressive rock. He told Mike Mettler of *Digital Trends* in August 2017 that, despite being proud of his previous records, 'if there's one thing I can say I might be guilty about … is the conceptual element took over from the songwriting element and the melodic element.'

Wilson told Prichett that this album had groups of songs that share a theme, and 'actually the whole record has a kind of underlying theme going on, if you choose to find it.' But he told Paul Sinclair of *Super Deluxe Edition* in August 2017 that 'one of the worst things you can do is go looking for concepts … I think this album is more like a book of short stories … rather than a novel.' And he told Anil Prasad of *Innerviews* in 2017 that 'there's a strong lyrical strand ... so it has a unity without it being conceptual.'

If there is a broad concept or theme, it's the state of the world as Wilson saw it when writing the album. In August 2017, he told Michael Hann of *Prog,* 'We've had Brexit, we've had Donald Trump, we've had the terrorists come right to our very doorstep, we've had Bataclan [the massacre in 2015], we've had Manchester [the arena bombing in 2017].' He felt it would be strange if the album did not at least touch on those events, although he told Mettler that he didn't want to make the album too overtly political: 'If you make [the songs] very political and very topical, it's going to date very quickly.' Instead, he wanted to create songs about 'characters that are living through these things' to provide a more universal and timeless appeal to human emotions.

There seem to be songs that can be grouped together by theme. There are two songs about politics ('To The Bone', 'The Same Asylum As Before'); one about immigration/refugees ('Refuge'); two about terrorism ('The People Who Eat Darkness' and 'Detonation'); two about the current state of the world but with hope for the future ('Nowhere Now' and 'Song Of Unborn'), loosely linked to one about escapism and pure joy ('Permanating'); and three about relationships ('Pariah', 'Blank Tapes' and 'Song Of I').

The underlying theme is truth, and the way it can be seen through different perspectives and sometimes distorted, whether by politicians, terrorists, or people in a relationship. The joyful songs view the world from a distance, which has the effect of mitigating some of the depressing concerns about the state of the world that are expressed elsewhere. But despite the brief moments of joy, the prevailing mood is one of anger and bitterness.

Wilson told Pratchett that the album's title refers to him 'getting back to the very core of my musical personality ... the songwriting side ... stripping away some of the more conceptual elements.' As a result, it's much more of a solo album, with Wilson playing most of the instruments himself rather than working with a de facto 'band' – as he had on the previous two albums – who provided virtuosic solo work that Wilson himself didn't attempt to match.

Wilson decided he needed a co-producer, and he chose guitarist and producer Paul Stacey, who has worked with Oasis and Noel Gallagher's High Flying Birds. Wilson told Prasad that Stacey was 'essential to the project.' They worked intensively together for three months in Paul's studio, which is packed with vintage gear. They can be seen at work, with various guest musicians, on the *Ask Me Nicely* documentary filmed by Lasse Hoile. Paul Stacey's identical twin, Jeremy, plays drums on the album. Jeremy Stacey has worked with Sheryl Crow and Noel Gallagher's High Flying Birds. He's also a guitarist, keyboard player and producer and has played drums and keyboards with King Crimson's touring band since 2016.

'To The Bone' (6:41) (Lyrics by Andy Partridge)

The album opens with a spoken-word intro by an American schoolteacher, Jasmine Walkes. She also runs a website called *Rumors And Riots Photography*. She has photographed Wilson on several live tours and provided additional photography for the *Get All You Deserve* DVD in 2012. Wilson told Mike Mettler he had given Walkes the basic theme of 'truth as a perspective', and she had improvised around it, providing something that was 'very natural, and not scripted'. The idea is that we now live in an era of 'post-truth' politics: 'Truth is an individual calculation, which means we all have different perspectives. There isn't one singular truth, is there?' The idea is that objective truth no longer exists, or if it does, it no longer has any value or meaning. Although it's unclear exactly when the term 'post-truth' was first used, by 2016, it had become so prevalent in discussions about politics that Oxford Dictionaries in the UK chose it as their Word of the Year.

In an interview with Stephen Humphries, posted on Wilson's website in August 2017, he explained this track is 'a cry from the heart to get right down to the bone and find out what the reality of a situation is, and if there is some truth to be found at the core.' Although the sentiments are clearly Wilson's own, the lyrics were actually written by Andy Partridge, founder of the English rock band XTC. In February 2016, Wilson told Greg Prato of *Songfacts* that 'Andy Partridge is one of my favourite songwriters of all time ... every song he writes has a very strong concept or idea behind it.' Wilson told Anil Prasad that he chose Partridge because the song 'needed to reference the world of politics and that's not something I'm really good at.' It was the first time Wilson had written a song with someone else's lyrics since the very early days of Porcupine Tree, when he had used Alan Duffy's on some of the songs from *On The Sunday Of Life* (1992) and *Up The Downstair* (1993).

There are some unusual lyrics, particularly the poetic lines 'Truth is the icy stream we dream about/Drinking from', which could have been written by one of the English Romantic poets like Wordsworth or Coleridge. And there appear to be Biblical references in the line 'Virgin, whore and crone'. On *Genius.com* in 2018, Jared Bissenden said that the three women are 'The Virgin Mary, the Whore of Babylon [from the Book of Revelation] and Malleus Maleficarum (The Hammer of Witches) [a treatise on witchcraft] for the crone.'

The song opens with the soulful sound of Mark Feltham's harmonica. Wilson was clearly referencing the classic art rock sound of bands like Talk Talk, whose lead singer Mark Hollis died in 2019. Feltham played on their classic albums *The Colour Of Spring* (1986), *Spirit Of Eden* (1988) and *Laughing Stock* (1991). He's a member of the English blues band Nine Below Zero and has an extensive discography as a session musician.

Low, ominous notes of a baritone electric guitar join the harmonica and a looped female voice (Ninet Tayeb), creating a sense of grandeur and unease. There's a hint of a Middle Eastern scale to the melody on the words 'truth is the icy stream'. Tayeb joins the verse, an octave higher than Wilson. Throughout the song, Wilson's guitar playing is more direct and edgy than on previous albums, probably due to his use of the Fender Telecaster (see 'People Who Eat Darkness', below). The guitar solo is very different from the soaring virtuosity that players like Guthrie Govan bring to other Wilson albums, but he still makes the guitar speak and move effectively, despite often denying he's a good musician. The song ends with a gorgeous coda, the spiky, almost funky nature of the rest of the song suddenly washed away by epic vocals and chords drenched in reverb as truth rains down. A final low note from the baritone guitar brings us back to Earth.

'Nowhere Now' (4:04)

Like 'Pariah' and 'Song Of Unborn', the verse and the chorus of this song describe polar opposites, at the extremes of pessimism and optimism. The title of the song has echoes of the Porcupine Tree song 'Arriving Somewhere But Not Here' (*Deadwing*, 2005).

We begin 'six feet underground'; humankind has lost its way, so we might as well be dead and buried. On Earth (or under it), we are moving backwards at the speed of sound, wasting our lives, failing to learn. Love no longer has any meaning. This contrasts with the chorus, in which the protagonist (a single individual rather than the collective 'we' of the verses) floats in space, feeling a 'rush' of the love that no longer exists on Earth. Looking down at Planet Earth, it appears 'luminous', the same joyous adjective that is used to describe the moon in 'Permanating'.

The track is very simple musically, which suits the relative simplicity of the concept and the optimism of the chorus. Adam Holzman plays understated piano and Hammond organ, and from the second chorus, the guitarist Dave Kilminster adds rich backing vocals. Kilminster has toured with Wilson and with Roger Waters. The guitar chords are straightforward, and the only concession to virtuosity is a few bars of graceful, flowing guitar in the instrumental break.

Structurally, the song is simple, too, but rather than ending on a fading chorus, it returns to the opening verse, and this, combined with the sombre piano outro, finally casts doubt on the optimism of the chorus.

Ken Grady of *Upside Adelaide* perceptively suggested to Wilson in September 2018 that there was a possible link between this song and David Bowie's *Space Oddity* (1969), which Wilson played live as a tribute to Bowie, who died in January 2016. Wilson reacted initially with slight surprise to Grady's suggestion, but soon accepted that he was right, as both songs share 'a sense of someone drifting high above the Earth, and seeing it as a beautiful thing far removed from all the politics and terrorism.'

The video was filmed by Lasse Hoile at the Atacama Large Millimeter Array, a collection of over 60 radio telescopes in the Atacama Desert in Chile.

'Pariah' (4:44)

At the time of writing, 'Pariah' is Wilson's most popular solo song on Spotify, with over 14 million plays. It's a duet between a pessimistic male character and a much more optimistic female character. The song shows that, as Walkes says in the spoken introduction to the album, there can be different perspectives on the same truth. On the Quora website in an undated post, Deepayan Ghosh provides a fascinating scientific analogy for the song, which 'moves in the form of a sinusoidal wave [a sine wave] alternating between two states of mind. Eventually, the song ends on a high note, and there seems to be a resonance in the mindwaves of these two beings...'

The dynamic between the two protagonists is very similar to the classic 1980s song 'Don't Give Up' by Peter Gabriel, a duet with Kate Bush. It was released as a single in October 1986 and reached number nine in the UK.

Both songs feature a depressed male protagonist in the verse and a female protagonist in the chorus, who urges him to 'begin again' and not to give up.

Gabriel's song is about depression caused by unemployment: 'For every job, so many men/So many men no-one needs'. Wilson's song is about another kind of outcast, a social outcast or pariah. The pariah has 'feet of clay', a Biblical image referring to Daniel's dream of the statue of King Nebuchadnezzar, which was made of precious metals at the top but shows human weakness by having feet made of clay, often used to describe the basic material from which humankind was formed. As a huge ABBA fan, Wilson may be unconsciously referencing the use of the phrase in 'Happy New Year' (*Super Trouper,* 1980). That song has a melancholy feel, far from the celebration that the title might suggest, and regards man as a fool dragging feet of clay.

Wilson admitted to Prasad that the line 'I'm tired of Facebook' is 'to a degree, autobiographical ... I am tired of everyone being a journalist and a critic.' But he also said that as a professional musician, he accepted that Facebook – and other social media platforms – can be very useful as a way of connecting with his fanbase 'so quickly, so easily and for free.'

The lines 'Well, being alone now/It doesn't bother me/But not knowing if you are/That's been hell you see' are so poignantly sung that they may be personal to Wilson himself. They are open to different interpretations. Tunaboy 45, in an undated post on *Genius.com*, takes a personal approach, referring to the heartbreaking interview in which Wilson admitted to being alone, Steven Wilson: I've Sacrificed Family For Music, posted by Jarrett Bellini on YouTube in January 2017. (As fans will know, Wilson has since married and has two stepchildren.) Tunaboy 45 says the words also reflect on Wilson's fears that you are never truly alone 'in this digital world where everything you do is tracked and everyone knows where you are at all times.' In July 2017, OctaneTwisted (adopting the name of Porcupine Tree's 2012 live album) refers to the fact that the protagonist 'has pushed his loved one so far away that now he can't even know of their well-being.' This interpretation removes Wilson from the picture. Another interpretation, again personal to Wilson, could refer to the traumatic breakup he had, which lurks behind some of the Porcupine Tree songs. The lines could then mean that he has finally got over the breakup and is happy to live alone, but not knowing whether his former partner (the 'you' of line three) has found another partner still causes immense jealousy.

The final words of the song have also caused comment online. They are sung by the male protagonist, as he asserts that there is no need to worry now because 'nothing really dies/Nothing really ends'. OctaneTwisted says this means that the protagonist's love for his loved ones will never die. On *Genius.com*, in January 2018, ArmasWeselius said, 'The lines are almost too optimistic, up to a sort of naiveness.' Whichever interpretation is correct – and they are both good – the ending is as beautiful as the rest of the song.

This is the first of two songs on the album in which Wilson duets with Ninet Tayeb, the other being 'Blank Tapes'. Wilson told Ezell that he was writing specifically with her in mind, so 'she changed the writing process for me, given that I knew the musical skill she is capable of.' In *Ask Me Nicely (The Making Of To The Bone),* Wilson can be seen duetting face-to-face with Tayeb.

This song segues from the previous one, opening with glittering synth arpeggios that create a sense of mystery. Strummed acoustic guitar soon joins in, and there's subtle piano from Holzman. The track has a huge dynamic range, as the emotions of the song pass from gentle melancholy to an epic instrumental section in which rising guitar chords create a sense of joy, which is mitigated by the fact that they are mostly in a minor key. The end of the song drops right back down to the intimacy of the beginning, with Wilson gently strumming an acoustic guitar to accompany his voice. The final chord progression doesn't really resolve (ending with a so-called imperfect cadence), leaving the song feeling unfinished to reflect the final sentiment 'nothing really ends'.

The video, shot by Hoile, concentrates on the faces of the two singers, separately, as they address each other. It's mostly black and white with a photographic negative effect, but it bursts into colour for about a minute at around 3:17. It perfectly captures the heartfelt simplicity of the song, and it has deservedly become one of Wilson's most viewed videos.

'The Same Asylum As Before' (5:14)

Wilson told Grady that the idea behind the song is quite simple: 'It doesn't matter who you vote for … you're still stuck with the same madhouse that you were before.' The use of the word 'asylum' as a metaphor may date back to 1919 when prominent film actors and directors formed their own film distribution company, United Artists. The Producer Richard Rowland is alleged to have coined the phrase 'the lunatics have taken over the asylum' in response to the idea of industry practitioners taking power from those who run it. The phrase has come to mean the people least capable of running an organisation have taken charge – not true in the case of United Artists, which was very successful.

It's interesting that the word 'asylum', originally meaning a place of refuge for those in physical or mental pain, has been linked with the word 'lunatic' in the public imagination. The next song on the album, 'Refuge', is about asylum-seekers who seek political asylum or refuge.

Musically, the song is a miniature anthem, starting with a rocky guitar. Wilson sings high falsetto in the verse, a vocal technique he developed with great success on the next album, *The Future Bites*, having used it only rarely on his previous records. The chorus yet again demonstrates Wilson's ability to write a catchy pop hook, something which he has done throughout his lengthy career – critics who have branded him niche, difficult, or an acquired taste seem to have overlooked this.

A lively middle eight, with guitars flying round the stereo picture and up and down the octave, leads to a more stately, spacious instrumental section with a bluesy, almost Floydian guitar solo, dating back in style to the very early days of Porcupine Tree when Wilson played psychedelic space rock. Towards the end, strings from the London Orchestra add to the song's epic richness.

The video was shot by Hoile. According to the notes on YouTube in January 2019, it was shot mostly in the woods in Denmark. It features two men with artificial heads, 'Woodface' and 'Perturbed big-head guy'. The latter is terrorised by the former, as satire passes into horror. The character of Woodface, a blank-faced character wearing evening dress and with branches instead of hands, also appears in the video for 'Harmony Korine' (*Insurgentes*).

'Refuge' (6:42)

Wilson told Humphries the song is about the refugee crisis in late 2015, when refugees attempted to smuggle themselves through the Channel Tunnel into the UK. He said that some had died in their attempt. (According to the BBC News website, 13 died between late June and early October 2015). He also referred to the refugee camps in Calais (known as 'the Jungle') in which human beings were living in 'the worst possible conditions, incredible squalor.' Wilson said he wasn't trying to make a political point but to write about the 'human side' of the crisis and the power of the human spirit to transcend the most dangerous conditions.

Lyrically, the song is as simple and moving as it could possibly be – the plight of the refugees speaks for itself without complex poetry. Wilfred Owen, the English First World War poet, quoted by composer Benjamin Britten in the score for *War Requiem* (1962), wrote, 'the poetry is in the pity … all a poet can do today is warn.' The music reflects this simplicity. Wilson told Mettler that 'it's pure production, very simple in a way – taking a song that's very simple on paper and painting it with sounds, colours and layers.'

The song opens with an arpeggiated synth line, which Wilson programmed on the Sequential Prophet-6, one of a few keyboards he bought to inspire him to write the album. He told Humphries that when he had written the pattern, he 'stepped up to the piano and played chords over the top.'

The song has a very unconventional structure. It begins with a few simple chords, based on the Lydian mode, that pivot beneath introspective vocals. At 2:00, Wilson's voice suddenly leaps into stratospheric falsetto. In May 2018, he told Fabrizio Pedrotti that he found his upper vocal register was getting stronger as he exercised it more, like any muscle. He was writing songs for the album when Prince died, and was strongly influenced by his use of falsetto: 'Maybe I'm not a black funky guy from Minneapolis, but singing like that is a way to keep myself evolving.'

The falsetto leap marks the start of a guitar-driven passage, and the vocals become more impassioned when the protagonist thinks of his wife and children. The passage that follows is the most unconventional section in the song, an instrumental breakdown where solos follow each other almost as they would on a jazz record – Feltham's bluesy harmonica solo, an improvised guitar solo from Wilson's co-producer Paul Stacey and, finally, a keyboard solo. Wilson told Humphries that the keyboard sound was inspired by Robert Wyatt's 1970s albums, such as *Rock Bottom* (1974): 'It has a slightly wavy quality as if it's coming from a faulty tape-recorder ... I love sounds with that tremulous quality.'

The track ends with a long outro, featuring the electronic soundscapes of the start, with haunting piano chords and subdued harmonica. There's a quiet, passionate plea for a return to normal life: 'Will you give back to me now/What you stole?' The final piano chord is a major seventh in G rather than a straight chord of G major, leaving the end questioning and ambiguous.

'Permanating' (3:35)

This song is shot through with pure joy, something very unusual in Wilson's back catalogue. To find another Wilson song that might raise a smile, you have to go as far back as the bouncy, eccentric joy of 'Linton Samuel Dawson' from the Porcupine Tree album *On The Sunday Of Life,* 25 years earlier. But it hasn't been for want of trying on Wilson's part. He told Grady that 'writing a simple, direct piece of joyous pop music is ... the hardest thing of all to do ... it may be the first and last time I ever managed to pull it off!' As he has often said, he grew up listening to Pink Floyd, but added that he also listened to 'the joyous pop music of artists like ABBA and The Bee Gees.' In the September 2017 issue of *Uncut* magazine, Wilson listed *ABBA Gold* (1992) as one of his favourite albums: 'To me, the ABBA catalogue is peerless in terms of the quality of songwriting, the crafting of pop melodies and pop production.' He said to make great pop songs, you need to listen to ABBA, The Beatles and The Beach Boys. He told Prasad that he hoped 'Permanating' could sit alongside classics like ELO's 'Mr Blue Sky' (1978) and ABBA's 'Mamma Mia' (1975). The cheerful opening piano chords sound like an ABBA song, and the uplifting guitar solo sounds like ELO. He told Sinclair of *Super Deluxe Edition* that '25 years ago, there's no doubt in my mind that [it] would have been a big hit, but we live in a very different world.'

Not all Wilson's fans enjoyed the track. On the tour to promote the album, he prefaced it with a speech encouraging the audience to stand up and dance to it. He was aware of the criticism the song generated online. As he said to Ezell, he'd heard that most of the comments were positive, but 'it's always the 10% of people that are unhappy and shout the loudest that make the biggest splash.'

The vibrant video, directed by Andrew Morgan, features Wilson playing an upright piano, surrounded by smiling Bollywood dancers with beautifully bright costumes. He told Prasad that on the original version, he was playing the piano in a public place, and was joined by flash mob dancers. The plan was to film the amused reactions of passers-by, but the documentary feel didn't work, so instead Wilson went for the 'magic' of shooting it 'in a cinematic way', full of glamorous costumes. Prasad asked Wilson a very astute question about using Bollywood dancers in a video that doesn't feature any Indian music. This raises the issue of cultural appropriation, but Wilson's reply was robust, 'not being too reverential or hung up on cultural authenticity is what artists have always done.' Or, to put it more directly, 'I was just trying to make something fun…'

Holzman plays keyboards on the album version. Wilson told Prasad that he was worried about asking Holzman to play the 'almost mechanically repetitive piano part … but ... he loved doing it.'

'Blank Tapes' (2:09)

This song, like 'Pariah', is a duet with Tayeb. It's a deliberately stark contrast with the joy of the previous song and the jolting violence of the next. It's a beautiful, melancholy breakup song, of which Wilson has written many over the years. Wilson told Humphries that the demo was more complicated, with additional acoustic guitars, a banjo and vocal treatments. He stripped down the final version, leaving only 'a single guitar, piano, [the] two voices and a couple of Mellotron overdubs.' The piano part was played by Holzman, with 'an almost painterly quality.' The sparse arrangement allows us to concentrate on the two voices in the song. All that's left of the relationship between the two protagonists is the blank tapes in her car – as ozymadandias42 said in May 2018 on *SongMeanings.com*, the song refers to the 'outdated romantic concept of making music tapes [mix tapes] as a sign of love.' Their erasure is a metaphor for the loss of love.

'People Who Eat Darkness' (6:03)

The title of this song could come from the non-fiction book *People Who Eat Darkness: Love, Grief And A Journey Into Japan's Shadows* (2010) by Richard Lloyd Parry. The author told Susan K Perry of *Psychology Today* in June 2012 that 'In Japanese, 'eating darkness' means flirting with the dark side.' Whether or not Wilson was aware of the book, it's a powerful image, memorably captured by Jess Cope in the video in which one of the characters appears to eat a black cat.

Wilson told Humphries that this song was written in response to the terror attack at the Bataclan concert venue in Paris. Wilson himself has played there, both with Porcupine Tree and as a solo artist. On Friday 13 November 2015, as part of a series of attacks across Paris coordinated by Islamic State, gunmen fired into the crowd at a concert by the Californian rock group Eagles of Death Metal. The gunmen killed 89 people, and at least 99 others were critically injured. Humphries asked Wilson whether it made him more worried about playing live gigs. Wilson replied that terrorism could happen 'anytime, anywhere'.

The song is about the terrorist who lives next door, and the almost clichéd response of neighbours in media interviews – 'he seemed like a normal, nice young man. Who could possibly know that they were so full of hatred, rage and darkness?' The only contact between the terrorist and his next-door neighbour is 'the slightest nod as we're passing on the stairs'. After a terrorist act, society may take the blame even though it's not really society's fault: 'You're penitent maybe/But it's not your fault you fail to see'. This doesn't address the wider failure in some cases of the security forces to follow potential terrorists who have been identified as a possible threat, but Wilson isn't making a political point here. He doesn't attempt to explore or justify the terrorist's motivations, except in the most general way. The protagonist addresses society in general – 'You tell me how to live/And you feed me with your poison 'til I'm sick' – but there is one moment of tender insight at around 2:50 when the point of view changes and the narrator directly addresses the terrorist: 'Well you lost control/And your kids became confused'. This reveals that the terrorist has become trapped with nothing left to lose: 'So now your chickens/Are coming home to roost'. The contemplative nature of this passage contrasts with the brutal anger of the rest of the song.

The track features a much more direct, crunchy guitar sound than on previous albums. Like many others on the album, it features the Fender Telecaster. Previously, Wilson had often used PRS (Paul Reed Smith) guitars, but when he started writing this album, his other guitars were out on the road.

The guitar he used is a Fender Telecaster Custom Shop 1963 Relic in black with a rosewood fingerboard. He told Humphries it had been sitting in the corner of his room, virtually unplayed. He picked it up and 'suddenly found a new way of playing.' He explained to A. Lee Graham of *Classic Rock Revisited* that the Telecaster sound is 'very wiry, very trebly ... it has that Pete Townshend slashing quality to it.' This led him to think about guitar parts in a different way – if he had stuck with his PRS guitar, it would have 'taken it down a metal sound, but a Tele is more punky, slashy.' This was the first song he wrote for the album, and changing guitars marked a major change in style. Wilson told Humphries that by playing most of the instruments on this track himself, he could make it sound 'a bit unschooled and punky', whereas in the past, it could have been a band effort that 'might have sounded too good!'

Cope's video retains the song's dark energy, but as she explained on *YouTube* in October 2018, she became worried that the 'Manchester arena bombing happened, and it stopped me in my tracks.' As the video was to be shown at Wilson's live shows, she decided she wanted something less literal, so 'terrorism turned into an alien invasion.' The look of the video was inspired by the 1998 science fiction horror film *The Faculty* and also by Alfred Hitchcock's *Rear Window* (1954).

'Song Of I' (5:22)

Wilson told Humphries he was astonished but happy that the record company chose this song as a single: 'The idea that they think it might actually be played on the radio is amazing to me.'

The song is about a dangerous obsession within a relationship. The protagonists can give up everything except each other – the song's title suggests that this isn't a sign of altruism, but rather an expression of supreme egotism and an obsession with another based on self-obsession. Wilson told Humphries that the idea of never giving someone up could be 'a very romantic sentiment, but it could also be a very creepy one depending on the context.'

In *Uncut* magazine, Wilson described the sound as 'sexy sinister', the kind of thing you hear on Depeche Mode's 'Personal Jesus' from *Violator* (1990), which he listed as one of his eight favourite albums. He also said he was influenced by 'I Feel You' (*Songs Of Faith And Devotion,* 1993). The whipcrack of percussion may imply some perverse sexual practice, woozy synthesisers suggest the blinding effect of obsession and sleazy strings show the relationship is far from healthy. The whole song is a miniature, very effective film noir.

Wilson told Graham the song is 'about love going from a very positive thing to a very destructive thing.' He wanted it to be a 'gender-neutral song sung by both male and female voices.' He decided not to use Tayeb, his usual duet partner, as her voice is 'very earthy, organic, powerful [and] emotional.' Instead, he chose Swiss singer-songwriter Sophie Hunger, who was recommended by his record label. Her coolly sensual approach is perfect for the track. She doesn't appear in the video for the song, however. Instead, Wilson chose Maya Petrovna, who describes herself on her website as 'an operatic 'crossover' alto, film music composer, multi-instrumentalist and physical theatre performance artist.' Wilson told Clive Morgan of *The Telegraph* in August 2017 that he wanted the video to represent the song as 'some form of highly stylised drama ... between choreography and soap opera.'

'Detonation' (9:20)

Wilson told Prasad this song was inspired by the 2016 terrorist attack on the Pulse Nightclub in Orlando, Florida. Omar Mateen shot and killed 49 people. According to the BBC News website, Islamic State claimed responsibility for the attack, but it was unclear to what extent Mateen was acting alone. President Obama said at the time there was 'no evidence yet of any contact between the gunman and Islamic State' – it appeared to be an act of 'homegrown extremism' inspired by content Mateen had seen online. Wilson told Prasad there was a strong suggestion that Mateen was acting alone, but that 'he used the idea of a religious war as some kind of badge to justify his actions to himself and the rest of the world.' Wilson was concerned that such people used a perceived link to a 'religious fundamentalist organisation' to justify their actions, and decided to write a song about one of those people. He told Humphries that 'some people are now turning to religion as a way to disguise their own self-loathing and mental illness.' This is perfectly captured in the lines, 'Great God I don't believe in you, but I will do what you want me to.'

This isn't the first time Wilson has expressed concern about shootings in America. When discussing the Porcupine Tree album *Fear Of A Blank Planet* (2007), a major theme of which was the disaffection of teenagers, he referred to the access they had to guns and, in particular, the massacres at Columbine (April 1999) and Virginia (April 2007).

Like 'Refuge', which, in some ways, is a mirror image thematically, the song has an unusual structure. It's the longest track on the album, and the extended instrumental section at the end, heavy with guitar, makes it one of the very few songs which could be described as prog rock (although this is a label about which Wilson is ambivalent at best).

It opens with disturbingly uneven percussion, perhaps representing the protagonist's disturbed state of mind. The guitar arpeggios that follow are played with a clean guitar tone, and the atmosphere at first is innocent enough, including a strangely lyrical chord progression under the words 'and the ones that are given it all/The good looks, the wealth/and the charm and the innocence' that could have come from a musical. But the heavily distorted spoken words 'But I will take it back' warn that something much darker is coming. They are similar in tone to the spoken words on Pink Floyd's 'One Of These Days' (*Meddle*, 1971): 'One of these days I'm going to cut you into little pieces'. The sentiment in 'Detonation' is equally bleak: 'Detonation for the greater good'.

Wilson told Prasad that the second half of the song, a funky groove which pivots between two chords in G minor and E minor, was inspired by the track 'Dream Within A Dream' from German synthpop band Propaganda's first album *A Secret Wish* (1985), which has 'a cinematic section with two chords going around.' But the addition of a virtuosic guitar solo by the Slovak guitarist and film music composer David Kollar took the track away from the 'almost Trevor Horn ZTT groove thing I intended', turning the track into more of a prog rock epic than originally planned. Kollar was recommended to Wilson by King Crimson drummer Pat Mastelotto. Wilson said, 'I wanted something about it to be fresh and modern, and David nailed it ... it's difficult to place what genre it's coming from.'

'Song Of Unborn' (5:56)

Wilson often ends his albums with a melancholy ballad, but although this song is also a ballad, its message is positive and uplifting. Wilson told Prasad that if the world is a place where there are 'terrorists, politicians who lie, refugee crises and religious fundamentalists', it's hard to understand why anyone would want to be born into that world. He said he 'wanted some positivity on this record', and the song has a very simple message: 'You can do something extraordinary with your life.' Wilson told Fabrizio Pedrotti that the song is also anti-religious: 'For religions, it is good to suffer in life because you supposedly go and find God after death.' His song instead celebrates the fact that in life, 'we all have the opportunity to do amazing things.'

The song is similar to 'Nowhere Now' and 'Pariah' in expressing opposite viewpoints, with the positive winning through. It addresses an unborn child who will face a dystopian future when 'the cities are lost to rain'. But there is hope amongst the wreckage: 'The arc of your life/Could still be profound'.

It opens with very quiet spoken words that suggest that there has been a change of tone to something more positive, 'Wait, something happened', heavily echoed, before the piano ballad begins. At around 1:45, the song stops completely with a moment of spacey electronics as we hear the fast heartbeat of the unborn baby, followed by the low drumbeat of the mother's heart as the song restarts. An ethereal choir part, arranged by Wilson himself and performed by Synergy Vocals, adds to the song's luminous beauty. According to Patrick McAfee, reviewing the album for *DPRP* in August 2017, the song features 'choral moments that feel respectfully similar to Kate Bush's 'All The Love' (from *The Dreaming,* 1982). Wilson told Humphries the choir arrangement is 'almost pagan in its beauty and optimism.' There's an echo of the wordless choirboy who appears on *Hand. Cannot. Erase*. The song reaches a climax on the words 'Don't be afraid to die/Don't be afraid to live' that express the opposites of death and life, the song having progressed from a slow piano ballad to an epic hymn. The song ends on a life-affirming statement – 'Don't be afraid' – confirmed by a strong chord of E major, which brings a positive resolution, a beautiful end to the album.

Cope's gorgeous video doesn't follow the song in detail or attempt to create its own narrative. In the YouTube notes, Cope says she was inspired by a quote from American professor of astronomy and author Carl Sagan: 'We are all made of star stuff.' She aimed to create an image of 'the evolving foetus in utero.' Fish are used as visual metaphors to represent sperm, blood cells and nerves. Whales, creatures that can survive underwater like fish but are also air-breathing mammals, represent the birth of a child as it leaves its mother's womb and takes its first breath.

Compilations

Unreleased Electronic Music (2004)

Personnel:
Steven Wilson: all instruments
Theo Travis: saxophone on 'Nailbomber'
Recorded at No Man's Land, Hemel Hempstead
Producer: Steven Wilson
Release date: on CD-R as Unreleased Electronic Music Vol. 1 (April 2004), on LP as Unreleased Electronic Music (November 2005) and on CD (March 2017)
Chart placings: did not chart
Running time: 65.32
Record label: Headphone Dust (UK), Tonefloat (Netherlands)
Current edition: unavailable

In 2004, Wilson mined his experimental archive for unfinished projects and released them on two limited-edition CD-Rs titled *Unreleased Electronic Music Vol. 1*. Each copy contained an original Polaroid photograph taken by Lasse Hoile. The run of only 350 copies sold out quickly and soon became a collector's item. The album was re-released on vinyl as a two-LP set on Tonefloat, including an additional track – a remix of 'Shortwave' – and again on CD-R. In 2017, a full CD version was released on Headphone Dust. Volume 2 was never released, so 'Vol. 1' was dropped from the title.

In the sleeve notes, Wilson says that despite a long and successful career in rock music, 'my real love might just be electronic music.' Those who only know Wilson for his work with Porcupine Tree and his solo albums may be surprised to hear that he grew up listening to German electronic artists such as Klaus Schulze and Tangerine Dream (whose work he later remixed) and the experimental composer Karlheinz Stockhausen. He goes on to list several other electronic artists he came across in the 1990s, including Aphex Twin (Richard James), whose EP *Digeridoo* (1992) he quotes as 'an epiphany of sorts.' *Unreleased Electronic Music* is proof of not just Wilson's love of electronic music but his extensive experiments with it, which found an outlet in his Bass Communion ambient project. This album consists mostly of electronic dance music, whereas his other electronic album, *Tape Experiments*, is mostly ambient. Wilson admits that some of the pieces are abandoned experiments, 'not all of it works.' Intriguingly, though, he invites the careful listener to follow the electronic thread of his musical personality into his other music.

'King Of The Delta Blues' (4:40)

The sleeve notes say this track and 'To Wear A Crown' were 'made in collaboration with Chris Lewis', the guitarist with Crashing Time who gigged with No-Man. Wilson wrote the rhythm track 'with lots of very aggressive distortion and compression', and Lewis provided processed guitar parts.

'Observer Commercial' (0:56)
The first of three TV adverts on this compilation. As Wilson told Dave Simpson of *The Guardian* in August 2017, 'the irony is that those journalists who've never heard of me were hearing my music all the time ... it was all over TV in the 1990s.'

In the sleeve notes, he says that in the mid-1990s, 'every TV commercial producer wanted something that sounded like either Chemical Brothers, 'Born Slippy' by Underworld, or The Prodigy.'

Music for other adverts is also available on the CD that comes with the second volume of the Special Edition of Wilson's 2022 book, *Limited Edition Of One*. The other companies he wrote for are represented by the tracks 'CDnow (online store)', 'DMX digital radio', 'Ford Fiesta', 'Lyons Maid Solero' (although the Solero ice cream is actually made by Wall's), 'McVities (biscuits)' and 'Sony PlayStation'.

'Dub Zero' (8:09)
Chris Wild asked Wilson to remix one of the ambient techno tracks he released under the name Dub Zero. Wilson said he wanted to obliterate the original track, 're-arranging it to the point where it becomes a completely unique work.' He only kept 'the sounds and loops' from the original. In his view, this track has not dated well.

'The Tobogganist' (6:36)
Inspired by Rochdale electronic duo Autechre's 1995 EP *Anvil Vapre*, Wilson was planning to start another side project under the name The Tobogganist, but this was the only track he wrote for the album. In his own words, this was 'probably just as well.'

'Shortwave' (7:28)
Wilson said this began as 'a completely beatless ambient Bass Communion track.' He tried adding rhythms, but forgot about it until he was choosing tracks for this album.

'Telegraph Commercial' (1:00)
See 'Observer Commercial' above.

'To Wear A Crown' (5:09)
The second collaboration with Chris Lewis, the other being 'King Of The Delta Blues'.

'Nuclear Head Of An Angel' (5:20)
Wilson admitted that this doesn't really belong on a compilation of electronic music because all the sounds are made by acoustic guitar. It does, however, provide some respite from the 'more noisy beat-driven tracks.'

'Nailbomber' (4:14)
Referred to in the sleeve notes as 'Nail Bomber' [sic]. Originally an idea for a TV commercial, it was rejected by the client, so Wilson decided to reuse it during a jam session with saxophonist Theo Travis. Wilson provided live processing and manipulated the backing track to produce what he drily described as 'free jazz electronica.'

'Slut 1.4' (9:32)
Wilson said this was inspired by electronic duos Scorn (formed by Napalm Death members Mick Harris and Nic Bullen) and Techno Animal (Justin Broadrick of Godflesh and Kevin Martin of the band God). He made a few tracks in this style, 'dark, brooding downtempo tracks with semi-industrial beats', but decided his weren't as good as the originals.

'Apres-Mortes' (includes hidden track **'Virgin Commercial'**) (12:15)
Wilson said this was inspired by his early love of the music of Klaus Schulze and the Kosmische Musik of 1970s Germany. He described it as 'the prettiest and most accessible' song on the album, which is why, in his view, it has dated less than other tracks, apart from 'Nuclear Head Of An Angel'.

Tape Experiments 1985/1986 (2010)
Personnel:
Steven Wilson: all instruments, voices and production
Recorded at Wilson's home studio
Release date: UK: September 2010 (free download), Netherlands: November 2010 (LP)
Chart placings: did not chart
Running time: 37.20
Record label: Headphone Dust (download), Tonefloat (vinyl LP)
Current edition: unavailable
According to the Discogs website, the original plan was to release *Tape Experiments* as a free CD with the *Insurgentes* DVD. Instead, the DVD was released with the single 'Vapour Trail Lullaby' and *Tape Experiments* came out as a free download and as a vinyl LP. The tracks were recorded in 1985-1986 when Wilson was in his late teens.

The sleeve notes state that this album represents 'various attempts to make academic avant garde [sic] electronic music ... of historical interest only.' All tracks were recorded onto a four-track cassette machine, except the final two, which were recorded on two-track analogue tape.

The four-track machine (which can be seen on the cover) was built by Wilson's father and had no erase head. The two-track machine was a Philips P50, on which Wilson learned the almost-lost art of editing analogue tape with a razor blade. He also used a tape delay machine made by his father. (For more information, see 'Designing Sound', chapter 12 of

Wilson's book *Limited Edition Of One*). All quotations below are taken from the LP sleeve.

'Cries Of Lucia' (10:34)
Recorded by Wilson layering his voice through the echo/delay machine made by his father, the track was 'vaguely inspired' by *Visage* (1961), written by the Italian composer Luciano Berio for electronics and voice. On lucianoberio.org, *Visage* is described as 'almost a soundtrack for a play that has never been written ... [it] does not offer a meaningful text or a meaningful language.'

'Cries Of Lucia' is an ambient soundscape of Wilson breathing and singing various vowel sounds, with occasional recognisable chords. It has a certain atmospheric charm and is the precursor of the multi-layered backing vocals that are such a rich feature of his later work. It's fascinating to consider what Wilson's music would have been like if he'd continued to follow this experimental route.

Wilson's No-Man collaboration with Tim Bowness sampled parts of the track on 'Sinister Jazz' (*Wild Opera*, 1996) and it was also part of the 'sonic soup' that made up 'The Gospel According To The IEM' on Wilson's side-project *I.E.M.* album (1996).

'I May Be Some Time' (5:57)
This was 'very much influenced' by the avant-garde English composer David Bedford's *Rime Of The Ancient Mariner* (1975), a 'very eerie album' for organ. A Farfisa organ treated with varispeed was used to create 'the queasy effects.' The track also includes bursts of atonal piano and an electronic storm which sounds like 'A Saucerful Of Secrets' from Pink Floyd's 1969 album *Ummagumma*. It ends with a low drone and spoken words describing the Terra Nova expeditions to the South Pole (1910 – 1913) led by Captain Scott. The title refers to Captain 'Titus' Oates, who left the tent where his companions were, sacrificing himself by walking into a blizzard as he felt he was becoming a burden, saying, 'I am just going outside. *I may be some time.*'

'Constellation' (3:23)
Inspired by Tangerine Dream's *Zeit* (1972), 'the year zero of all ambient music.' A gentle ambient track, with a simple but haunting chord progression, hinting at Wilson's melodic songwriting over the following decades.

'Them No 1' (4:31)
This begins with an electronic recreation of the sound of a helicopter, or maybe an alien spaceship (perhaps referred to by the word 'Them' in the title). With its eerie, slow synths, it could be the theme tune to a horror film. It's given a touch of the avant-garde with 'random radio transmissions.'

'The Life And Times Of Sigmund Freud' (3:56)

The title was 'stolen' from an early Robert Wilson theatre piece, which premiered in 1969. It took Wilson two weeks to complete this four-minute piece, using the 'classic music concrete techniques' of Stockhausen, to create a complex montage with 'sometimes as many as nine or ten edits per second.' Wilson seems to be quoting himself at about 1:00 – the helicopter sounds very similar to the opening of 'Them No. 1'. There's also a touch of the avant-garde experimentation of John Lennon's 'Revolution 9' from The Beatles' *White Album* (1968).

'Wood Between Worlds' (5:12)

Recorded 'live', Wilson played a Farfisa organ through a tape delay machine, mixed with birdsong and other ambient sounds from his parents' garden, recorded via a microphone 'hanging outside the window.' It's heavily influenced by early Tangerine Dream, when their music was largely ambient before they embraced strongly rhythmic sequenced passages.

'Seen' (3:47)

Features layered guitars passed through a tape delay machine. It has the feel of some of Robert Fripp's more solo ambient guitar tracks, but Wilson says it was 'probably quite influenced' by John Martyn's 'Small Hours' (*One World*, 1977).

Cover Version (2014)

Personnel:
Steven Wilson: voice and instruments
Produced by Steven Wilson
Release date: June 2014
Chart placings: did not chart
Running time: 55:13
Record label: Headphone Dust (CD) and Tonefloat (7" single)
Current release: Kscope

Cover Version is a compilation of six singles released by Steven Wilson between 2003 and 2010. Each single had a cover on the A-side and an original Wilson composition on the B-side. According to his sleeve notes, they were recorded 'quick and dirty', without the high production values of his other solo material. He didn't name the band or artist that had recorded the original versions, so listeners had no preconceptions about the songs. He assumed that some would recognise songs by artists such as Prince, The Cure and ABBA, but 'not everyone grew up in England in the 1980s as I did!' He described the singles as 'the first steps in my career as a solo artist.'

Cover Version I (March 2003)

'Thank You' (Alanis Morissette) (4:39)

Written on a trip to India in 1997 after the enormous success of *Jagged Little Pill* (1995), Alanis Morissette's original starts and ends with glittering keyboards and continues with a fairly straightforward indie rock feel. The song describes the crises she faced and how she came to terms with them to achieve personal growth. Wilson's version is called 'Thank You', whereas the original was titled 'Thank U'. As the song was a huge worldwide hit, perhaps he changed the name to divert listeners from the original source. His version is much more contemplative, with simple strummed guitars, slow-moving piano chords and warm synth washes. It has a certain charm, slightly marred by the occasional tightening of Wilson's voice on higher notes.

'Moment I Lost' (Wilson) (3:12)
A gorgeous vignette, expressing yearning regret at the loss of a golden moment in the protagonist's life. It recalls Wilson's beautifully melodic songwriting on Porcupine Tree's *Lightbulb Sun* (2003). The song describes this moment as 'This will be the thing I treasure', but now it's gone, the memory is tinged with sadness. The nostalgic feel is heightened by the use of slightly wobbly-sounding piano, which reminds Wilson of the cassette tapes of his youth (see the entry for 'First Regret', the first track on *Hand. Cannot. Erase.*), and by the use of the Mellotron, another evocative sound for him.

Cover Version II (October 2004)
'The Day Before You Came' (ABBA) (5:06)
A 1982 single by ABBA describing the mundane life of the protagonist the day before her lover came into her life. Wilson turns the song into a gentle, thoughtful ballad with strummed acoustic guitars, soulful backing vocals and added Mellotron. He perfectly captures the melancholy that lies behind the glitter and polish of many of ABBA's best songs, showing his great admiration for the group's skilled songwriting.

'Please Come Home' (Wilson) (3:50)
A simple, plaintive address to a 'lost boy' asking him to come home to 'make me whole', a pre-echo of the same words used to such powerful effect nearly a decade later on the title track of *The Raven That Refused To Sing*. The song begins with understated piano chords typical of a ballad, soon joined by burnished strings. The melancholy guitar solo is limpid in tone.

Cover Version III (September 2005)
'A Forest' (The Cure) (6:04)
A single from The Cure's 1980 album *Seventeen Seconds*. Wilson's version is dreamier and more spacey, replacing the driving guitars of the original with electronics and heavily panned percussion, and occasional Mellotron sounds. Although it's very different from The Cure's original, it shares the same magical introspection.

'Four Trees Down' (Wilson) (3:33)
This continues the slightly eerie theme of the single's A-side. We are still in a wooded place, perhaps a graveyard, or maybe a forest, where the protagonist is buried. The title seems to refer to the position of the grave, four trees down from the entrance to the graveyard or forest. It's a quietly poignant ballad sung by the dead protagonist lying underground, regretting a lost life and opportunities: 'I had so much to say/The time just slipped away'. The protagonist has become part of nature as spring comes and 'Frail birds sing', and 'Warm earth weighs down in my lungs'. It makes an interesting comparison with 'The Unquiet Grave' (see below) in that, despite his regrets, the protagonist is happy to 'wait/Underground/I've got time'. Although the song's theme could be rather grim, the vocal delivery wins us over, and a sweet theme played on glockenspiel gives the song an innocent quality.

Cover Version IV (July 2006)
'The Guitar Lesson' (Momus) (4:03)
Written by the Scottish songwriter Nicholas 'Nick' Currie, also known as Momus. The song comes from his 1989 album *Don't Stop The Night*. Lyrically, it's very disturbing, depicting an inappropriate relationship between a guitar teacher and his pupil, a 12-year-old girl, similar to that between Humbert Humbert and 'Lolita' (also a 12-year-old girl) in the novel of the same name written by Vladimir Nabokov in 1955. As Wilson said on his website, the song 'may create some controversy with its subject matter, guaranteed to offend.' But he added, musically the song is 'also very beautiful, I think.'

'The Unquiet Grave' (15th century English Folk Song arr. Wilson) (6:57)
This is the only B-side in the collection that isn't an original Wilson composition, but he makes the song his own by taking a simple 15th-century English folk melody and almost burying it in brooding backing vocals. For comparison, on the version sung by English folk singer Nancy Kerr on *Eliza Carthy And Nancy Kerr* (1993), Kerr sings it with traditional folk inflections, whereas Wilson sings it straight. At times, it has a similar feel to the psychedelic folk of his Storm Corrosion collaboration with Mikael Åkerfeldt.

The ballad describes a young man sitting on his dead lover's grave, mourning her for 'a twelve month and a day'. He disturbs her peace, begging her for a kiss, and she tells him he should enjoy his life while he can. Talking to Anil Prasad of *Innerviews* in 2017, Wilson related the song to the tradition of murder ballads, songs 'about death and people being haunted by the ghosts of their loved ones or people they murdered.' He returned to the form on *The Raven That Refused To Sing* on 'The Pin Drop' and 'The Watchmaker'.

Cover Version V (July 2008)
'Sign 'O' The Times' (Prince) (3:55)
The lead single from Prince's 1987 album of the same name. Wilson first played it live in Vienna on 21 April 2016 as a tribute to Prince, who died that day. Wilson appeared on Jools Holland's show on BBC Radio 2 on 30 April, playing a live version of the song. Wilson's cover is very powerful, capturing the anger and austere nature of the original, with beefy synth bass, raging guitars and vocals heavily treated with electronics. At the end, the track is overcome by noise music, as were many of the tracks on *Insurgentes,* released later that year.

'Well You're Wrong' (Wilson) (3:35)
Sung by a rejected lover, who doesn't want to see 'anybody but you'. Having listed the reasons why the protagonist wants to be with his lover, he says that in not wanting to be with him, she is, to put it simply, 'wrong'. This is probably unhelpful, bearing in mind his lover has no feelings: 'there's nothing inside' her. Wilson has written many better songs about the breakup of relationships, and the track is mainly notable for his early use of falsetto, which became much more important (and stronger) on later albums such as *The Future Bites*. Perhaps coincidentally, it's paired with a song by Prince, whose falsetto style was a huge influence on Wilson.

Cover Version VI (February 2010)
'Lord Of The Reedy River' (Donovan) (5:03)
First released by Israeli duo Esther & Abi Ofarim in 1968. Donovan himself recorded it for the 1969 film *If It's Tuesday, This Must Be Belgium* and his 1971 album *HMS Donovan*. Welsh folk singer Mary Hopkin recorded it for her debut album *Post Card,* released in 1969 on The Beatles' Apple label and produced by Paul McCartney. Kate Bush released it as the B-side of her 1981 single 'Sat In Your Lap'.

The song is based on the Greek myth in which the god Zeus, in the form of a swan, rapes or seduces Leda. Donovan's version is sung from Leda's point of view, in which she 'fell in love with a swan'. Wilson's cover features gently strummed guitars and sparkling keyboards, with vocals so close-mic'd it feels like he's in the room. The guitar solo is very similar to the style of Mikael Åkerfeldt, with whom Wilson was working in 2010 on the Storm Corrosion project. In his book *Limited Edition Of One*, Wilson described Åkerfeldt's style of playing as 'Lonely Swede lost in the forest'. The song ends with lush, layered backing vocals that are so typical of Wilson's work that it feels like an original rather than a cover.

'An End To End' (Wilson) (5:12)
Lyrically, this song is similar to the tracks on *Insurgentes,* which have their own poetic, dream logic in lines like 'Insect heavy dawn/Find the spawn' that

defy conventional interpretation. It has a similar feel to 'Glass Arm Shattering', the final song on the Porcupine Tree album *Deadwing* (2005), which is also built on very simple chords. But 'An End To End' is harmonically unusual, sometimes going off in an unexpected direction, for instance at 2:18 on the words 'I will sing to you'. At 4:43, the piano harmony suddenly passes to a minor key and the song ends in a completely different key. An intriguing experiment.

Transience (2015)

Personnel:
For details, see the original albums except 'Lazarus' backing track:
Steven Wilson: vocals, acoustic guitar, keyboards
Nick Beggs: Chapman stick
Guthrie Govan: guitar
Adam Holzman: piano, Hammond organ
Marco Minnemann: drums
Recorded on tour in March 2015 with studio overdubs added in July 2015
Release date: September 2015
Chart placings: UK: 59
Running time: 62:23
Record label: Kscope

The cover describes this compilation as 'songs recorded between 2003-2015: an introduction to the more accessible side of Steven Wilson'. It features tracks from the first four studio albums: *Insurgentes* ('Harmony Korine', 'Significant Other', 'Insurgentes'), *Grace For Drowning* ('Postcard', 'Deform To Form A Star', 'Index'), *The Raven That Refused To Sing* ('The Pin Drop', 'Drive Home') and *Hand. Cannot. Erase.* ('Transience', 'Happy Returns', 'Hand Cannot Erase'). There's a cover of 'Thank You' by Alanis Morissette (see *Cover Version*) and a new recording of 'Lazarus', from Porcupine Tree's *Deadwing* (2005). The 2016 single 'Happiness III', from the mini-album *4½*, is also included. Most of the songs are around three to five minutes long – some have been shortened to make them more accessible.

This is the first of Wilson's albums (including those with Porcupine Tree) to feature an image of him on the cover with his eyes open, looking directly at the camera. He said on his website, 'For once, I have also given in to narcissism and put my face on the cover, without a gas mask or anything else obscuring it!' Even on *Cover Version* (released the year before), his eyes can barely be seen on the sketch of his face. On *Insurgentes,* he is wearing a gas mask. On *Grace For Drowning,* he has his back to the camera. The ghost on *The Raven That Refused To Sing* has no eyes, and the figure on *Drive Home* has none. Even on *To The Bone*, which came out later than *Transience*, Wilson's eyes are closed. In September 2018, he told Ken Grady of *UpsideAdelaide* that having a close-up of his face on *Transience* was the '[record] label's idea, not mine, but I thought it was a good one.'

The original release was a limited vinyl-only issue to coincide with the second leg of the *Hand. Cannot. Erase.* tour. The double LP had three sides with music on, the fourth being an etching of the handwritten sketches for the lyrics of 'Happy Returns'. The following year, it was issued on CD.

'Lazarus' (2015 Recording) (3:57)
A live recording from the first leg of the *Hand. Cannot. Erase.* tour. For full details of the original song, see the chapter on *Deadwing* in the book *Porcupine Tree On Track* (Sonicbond, 2021), also by Nick Holmes. The main difference between the two versions is the slide guitar on the later version played by Guthrie Govan in a country and western style.

A Limited Edition Of One (2022)
Personnel:
Steven Wilson: all vocals and instruments
The second volume of the Special Edition of Steven Wilson's book *Limited Edition Of One,* published in 2022, comes with a CD of early tracks*, A Limited Edition Of One*. Some of the solo tracks had already been released on *Tape Experiments 1985/1986* in 2010: 'Constellation', 'Seen', 'The Life And Times Of Sigmund Freud' and 'I May Be Some Time'. Some of the music for adverts was released on *Unreleased Electronic Music* in 2004. Previously unreleased tracks are as follows:

'Remembrance' (0:40)
The first Wilson release, recorded in mid-1981 when he was 13. It was released on a cassette-only compilation called *Dreams Of Reality* later that year by Broken Skull Tapes. It begins with a short police radio broadcast, then a long chord on a Farfisa organ with an improvised melody above.

'Wasteland' (2.24)
An instrumental for multitracked bass guitars. Recorded in March 1984 on the four-track tape machine Wilson's father built for him. He was 16 and already a proficient bass player. It sounds like a technical exercise until about 1:10 when an evocative melody is introduced, with hints of the subtle dissonance of early songs by The Cure. It finishes on a triumphant chord.

'Russia On Ice' (4:32)
This and the next track were recorded in June 1987, when Wilson was 19 and beginning to work on early Porcupine Tree material. According to his book, he was now earning enough from his day job at a computer company to afford an Ensoniq ESQ-1, an early form of music workstation with built-in synth sounds, a sequencer and a keyboard. The track is a hybrid of what Wilson describes as the 'doom rock' of bands like The Cure and Joy Division and the early Porcupine Tree sound – the vocal style in particular will be

familiar to those who know the albums he recorded under that name. Wilson liked the title so much that he reused it for a track with completely different lyrics and music, on the Porcupine Tree album ***Lightbulb Sun*** (2000).

'Next Stop Wonderland' (2:07)
The synthesised piano sound hasn't dated well, but this gentle piano ballad gives a glimpse of Wilson's later, more mature style. As he modestly says in his book, he was 'a very late bloomer … maybe I was just starting to get a bit better.'

EPs

STVN WLSN – NSRGNTS RMXS (2009)

See Insurgentes (2008) for personnel
Additional personnel:
'Harmony Korine' (David A. Sitek Magnetized Nebula Mix):
Stuart Bogie: tenor sax
Todd Smith: trumpet
'Salvaging' (Pat Mastelotto Mix):
Cenk Eroglu: Turkish Strings, v-grr, Ebow, synths, percussion
Markus Reuter: 'an abundance of basses'
Adrian Benavides: extra guitar
Pamelia Kurstin: theremin
Kimmo Pohjonen: accordion
Release date: June 2009 (physical editions), October 2009 (digital edition)
Chart placings: UK: 116, US: did not chart
Running time: 38:19 (CD), 15:02 (vinyl 12" single)
Record label: Kscope

NSRGNTS RMXS, released in June 2009, contains remixed versions of some of the tracks from Steven Wilson's first solo album, *Insurgentes* (2008). The vowels were removed from 'Steven Wilson – Insurgentes Remixes' to create the title, rendered on the front cover of the CD as *STVN WLSN – NSRGNTS RMXS*. Sensibly, the CD spine provided the full title, including vowels. A remix competition was launched in January 2009 for the track 'Abandoner'. Wilson chose eight of the resulting mixes and the winner, Łukasz Langa, was selected in a public vote that ended in May 2009.

The 12" single featured the first track from the CD, 'Harmony Korine (David A. Sitek Magnetized Nebula Mix)' and two remixes of 'Only Child' by Pat Mastelotto that don't appear on the CD but did appear on the digital download that was released later. Mastelotto also remixed 'Abandoner', which was available to download to inspire entrants to the remix competition.

CD Version

'Harmony Korine' (David A. Sitek Magnetized Nebula Mix) (5:14)

Remixed by David Andrew Sitek (from American rock band TV on the Radio) and Jneiro Jarel (American producer and DJ Omar Jarel Gilyard). This remix replaces the loose-limbed, relaxed drumming of Gavin Harrison from Porcupine Tree in the verse with trip hop rhythms and rasping tenor sax (Stuart Bogie) and trumpet (Todd Smith). In the second verse, the level of distortion on the backing track is pushed to the limit, giving the song a more intense feel. But the most radical change is in the chorus, where the chord structure beneath the vocals is completely changed, giving it a more optimistic feel. Towards the end of the track, there's an additional resonant synth line which drifts downwards to mark the end of the song.

'Get All You Deserve' (Dälek Mix) (7:44)

Remixed by MC Dälek and Mike Manteca from American hip hop band dälek. The first of two remixes of this song, the second being by Fear Falls Burning (see below). This mix strips out the piano part from the first couple of minutes and replaces it with mesmerising vocal samples, reminiscent of the multilayered backing vocals on the 1974 single 'I'm Not In Love' by English art rock band 10cc. At around 2:00, Harrison's drums are replaced by a resolute hip-hop beat. In the chorus, Wilson's voice, drenched in echo, is almost lost beneath the beat. From around 4:00, the song is largely instrumental, reaching a climax with military snare drums and heavy percussion flourishes. It continues in this style until near the end, unlike the original, which features an unrelenting descent into noise. The song ends with a brief fade, with some of the piano motif from the original song.

'Abandoner' (Engineers Mix) (4:46)

Remixed by British pop band Engineers, who were described on the record company website as 'Kscope's newest act' at the time. The first of two remixes of the song, the second being the Danse Macabre mix by Łukasz Langa (see below). The most significant change is the addition of piano chords in the opening section, and an extra piano motif at around 2:50, which can be heard again later in the track but much lower in the mix. This has the effect of grounding the track, as does the extra guitar in the rhythmic instrumental section from around 2:10. The vocals are given much clearer definition, starting on the left-hand side of the mix with an added hi-hat pattern, then moving to the right, giving a more intimate but less dream-like feel to the track.

'Salvaging' (Pat Mastelotto Mix) (8:36)

Remixed by drummers Pat Mastelotto (King Crimson) and Pat Manske (Rhythmic Statues). On his website, Mastelotto says that he changed the time signature of the song (which he refers to as 'Salvager') from 4/4 to 5/4 and slowed it down so that he could bring the vocals closer together; in his view, 'the lyrics were too far apart in Steven's version.'

Mastelotto has fun with this mix, as he does with the others (see below). His version begins with eerie electronic noises, played on the theremin by Pamelia Kurstin, which gradually resolve into the opening chord of the original. Thunderously funky bass parts, played by Markus Reuter on 'an abundance of basses', soon appear. As promised, the vocals are much closer together than on the original. From 1:30, there are brief additional string flourishes and some wayward basslines. The instrumental break from around 2:50 adds Turkish Strings, provided by Cenk Eroglu. As the instrumental section morphs into the quieter section with orchestral strings, Mastelotto adds extra vocals and an energetic percussion part, which completely changes the contemplative nature of the original. A high melody is added by what sounds like a theremin. Unlike some other remixers on this album, he embraces the 'noise' section at the end, removing the heavy drums from the original and replacing them with a bassline that spirals upwards forever – a suitably dystopian ending.

'Abandoner' (Danse Macabre Mix) (5:34)

Remixed by Polish musician and software engineer Łukasz Langa. The second of two mixes of this song, the first being by Engineers (see above). As a classically trained pianist, Langa may well have taken the title of his mix from 'Danse Macabre' (1874), an orchestral piece by French composer Camille Saint-Saëns. Wilson himself listened to all 200 or so entries to the competition, of which this was the winner. A mini website, hosted by Wilson's record label Kscope, allowed entrants to download individual parts (or 'stems') from the original song, including 'behemoth guitars' and 'evil piano'.

Langa brings his classical skills to this mix, completely transforming the track into an epic piano ballad. It begins with a deep synth intro, soon joined by insistent piano chords and complex percussion rhythms. Wilson's introverted vocals work well with the completely different mix, sounding more confident in this context. The track builds to a magnificent climax until, at around 3:00, there's a contemplative piano passage with syncopated, rolling drums and a free-flowing bassline, and at 4:15, a melodic string part is added. The distinctive sound of a vibraslap (a percussion instrument) at around 4:30 announces the final, climactic section.

'Get All You Deserve' (Fear Falls Burning Mix) (6:20)

Remixed by Dirk Serries (aka ambient musician Fear Falls Burning). The second of two remixes of the song, the first being by dälek (see above). The first two minutes of the song are only subtly different from the original. There is more echo on the piano, and processing is applied to Wilson's voice to make it feel less intimate, as if heard in a distant dream. At around 3:00, the track seems to be ending, as what sounds like a final chord is restated several times. Unlike the Dälek Mix, the descent into noise from the original track is retained, but without Harrison's powerful drumming. This ambient version contrasts with the other, more aggressive-sounding tracks on this album but retains the essence of the original.

12" Single

'Harmony Korine' (David A. Sitek Magnetized Nebula Mix) (5:14)

The first track on the CD version (see above).

'Only Child' (Pat Mastelotto 'Mix 3') (3:32)

'Only Child' (Pat Mastelotto 'Mix 1') (5:56)

Personnel: Adrian Benavides: bass ('Mix 3'), guitar ('Mix 1'); Markus Reuter: bass ('Mix 3'), guitar ('Mix 3'), voice ('Mix 3'), bass clarinet ('Mix 1'); Tony Levin: bass ('Mix 1'); Gavin Meets Sherman (Gavin Harrison): drums ('Mix 3'); Roine Stolt:

organ, Mellotron, slide Guitar ('Mix 1'); Sha (Stefan Haslebacher): bass clarinet ('Mix 1'); Sirenee (Renée Stieger): voice ('Mix 3') and ('Mix 1'); PK (25): voice ('Mix 3')

On his website, Mastelotto quotes an email from Wilson asking him to keep the original vocals from the song and 'reinterpret the song [as] if you'd been producing it. And keep it twisted!' Mastelotto's response was 'to really go nuts' and, with the help of bassist Markus Reuter, superimpose a new meter and tempo on the track by breaking it down into its smallest rhythmic elements. So, a song in 4/4 at 100 bpm would become a song in 6/8 at 75 bpm. Mastelotto originally planned to do three remixes of *every song* on the album, which explains why there were three versions of the song.

Despite Wilson asking him not to remove his vocals, Mastelotto did exactly that on 'Mix 3'. The only thing that the original track and 'Mix 3' appear to have in common is that both have a prominent bassline. But whereas the original has a smooth, majestic bassline that gives the song a sense of inevitability (as many of The Cure's basslines do), the remix has a series of jerky, frenetic lines that don't use the same notes as the original. 'Mix 3' has a fractured structure, with several brief breaks that add to the unsettling feel. At around 4.00, there's an interesting rhythmic effect, sometimes described as an 'auditory illusion', where it suddenly seems to be playing at half speed. Mastelotto used similar auditory illusions when playing drums for King Crimson, as on the track 'Sex Sleep Eat Drink Dream' from *Thrak* (1995), in which he and the band's other drummer, Bill Bruford, at one point play in two different time signatures at the same time, as Bruford explained to Trevor Cox in the BBC Radio 4 documentary *Auditory Illusions* in September 2019 (full disclosure: the author of this book produced the programme while working for the BBC).

Mastelotto's 'Mix 1' is equally radical and disjointed. Bruford told Cox that in King Crimson's music, there was always 'a sense of a threat of impending doom' and Mastelotto creates that mood here. It begins with what sounds like an ending, a very low bass note (similar in timbre to the low note that ends 'Happy' from Storm Corrosion's 2012 album of the same name, a collaboration between Wilson and Mikael Åkerfeldt of Opeth). The original track appears at 0:25, but it's destroyed after a few seconds by an explosion. There's another explosion at around 1:05 and the track falls apart on another few occasions until finally we hear a snatch of a human voice, sampled and used as a human beatbox. Wilson used much the same technique on 'Actual Brutal Facts' (from *The Harmony Codex*). The track ends with a Floydian guitar solo. Although the track is dark and dystopian, there's a strong impression that Mastelotto is having fun being so subversive.

Digital Download

Released on 12 October 2009, it collects all eight tracks from the CD and 12" single.

Additional Competition Track
'Abandoner' (Pat Mastelotto Mix) (5.07)
The mini website set up for the remix competition included free downloads of the Engineers' remix and the Pat Mastelotto mix of 'Abandoner' to inspire entrants. The Engineers' remix is track three on *NSRGNTS RMXS* (see above), but the Mastelotto mix was never released elsewhere. It opens with shimmering guitar. The rhythmic breathing that appears at 0:40 is another technique that Wilson used on *The Harmony Codex*, on 'Inclination'. At 1:00, a new, dirty-sounding bassline appears. At 1:20, the original Steven Wilson vocal tries to break into the track. The grungy, King Crimson-like backing track continues regardless of Wilson's attempts, and for a while, the two elements seem to exist in completely different musical universes, resolutely ignoring each other. Then, at 3:00, the high synth parts of the original finally succeed in breaking into the song. Of the eight lines of lyrics of the original song, five appear in the remix. It's significant that the words 'I am restless, I am lost' are left out, as they are an apt description of the remix – Mastelotto appears to be having fun again! The track ends with a fairground organ that seems to come from a fever dream.

Drive Home (2013)
Personnel:
Steven Wilson: vocals, keyboards, guitars, bass on 'The Holy Drinker'
Nick Beggs: bass, backing vocals, Chapman Stick on 'The Holy Drinker'
Guthrie Govan: lead guitar
Adam Holzman: keyboards
Marco Minnemann: drums
Theo Travis: flutes, saxophones, clarinet
The London Session Orchestra: strings, arranged by Dave Stewart
Produced and mixed by Steven Wilson
Associate producer: Alan Parsons
Recorded at East West Studios, Los Angeles, in September 2012; No Man's Land, Hemel Hempstead, and Hugenottenhalle Frankfurt, Germany, in March 2012
Release date: October 2013
Highest chart placings: UK: 68, US: did not chart
Running time: 50:24
Record label: Kscope
On Steven Wilson's website, the *Drive Home* 'video EP' is described as 'essentially a single from *The Raven That Refused To Sing*, but so much more!' The video disc contains the gorgeous, emotionally wrought and haunting Jess Cope videos for 'Drive Home' and 'The Raven That Refused To Sing', and four songs recorded live in Frankfurt on the *Raven* tour: 'The Holy Drinker', 'Insurgentes', 'The Watchmaker' and 'The Raven That Refused To Sing'. The audio-only material also includes a new song, 'The Birthday Party', and an orchestral version of 'The Raven'.

'The Birthday Party' (3:46)

Recorded live during the studio sessions for *The Raven That Refused To Sing,* the song is based on one of the ghost stories that appear in the Deluxe Edition book. In January 2013, the story was released on YouTube as a lyric video with an instrumental version of 'The Watchmaker'. In October of that year, the song itself was released on YouTube as an audio-only version to promote the *Drive Home* EP. The track is mostly instrumental, but there are a few lyrics near the end. In 2022, Wilson published the ghost story in the second volume of the Special Edition of his book, *Limited Edition Of One*.

The story is about a girl called Victoria. Her birthday party is her only chance each year to play her favourite game of hide and seek. When it's her turn to hide, she goes to the music room, in a remote corner of the house, never visited by her parents and even ignored by the maids. She hides herself under a dust sheet that covers the grand piano.

Victoria falls asleep and wakes to discover that she hasn't been missed. She falls asleep again and has strange dreams. When she wakes again, she's unsure whether she's been asleep for an hour or a month. Finally, she wakes again and she hears angry voices in the room, but not those of her family. So she decides to remain hidden.

Victoria remains hidden for months, then years, until the house falls silent. She decides it's time to come out of her hiding place. The house now looks very different. She doesn't recognise the people who live there or the style of their clothes. They look straight through her. She leaves the house and walks into a world that she only recognises from her dreams. The green and brown of the countryside has been replaced with grey concrete, crowded with vehicles and people. At the end of the story, it's revealed that the central character is Victoria's ghost.

The track itself is a lively, proggy instrumental, with keyboard parts that sometimes sound like Keith Emerson of Emerson, Lake & Palmer, and all the musicians showing their virtuosic qualities. Occasionally, the track drops out to a spacey section where we hear Wilson's distant voice, repeated on a loop, with a ghostly Mellotron, taking it into the world of Wilson's story.

'The Raven That Refused To Sing (Orchestral Version)' (7:29)

An orchestral version of the title track of the *Raven* album. In August 2013, part of this version was used in the trailer for the movie *Pompeii* (2014), from just over a minute in.

4½ (2016)

Personnel:

Steven Wilson: vocals, autoharp, guitars, bass, Mellotron, piano, percussion, synthesisers and samplers, virtual instruments
Dave Kilminster: guitar ('My Book Of Regrets' and 'Don't Hate Me')
Guthrie Govan: guitar ('Happiness III')

Nick Beggs: bass, Chapman Stick, backing vocals
Adam Holzman: Wurlitzer, Hammond organ, Minimoog, Fender Rhodes, piano
Craig Blundell: drums
Marco Minnemann: drums ('Happiness III')
Chad Wackerman: drums ('Sunday Rain Sets In')
Theo Travis: flute, saxophone
Ninet Tayeb: co-lead vocals on 'Don't Hate Me'
Produced and mixed by Steven Wilson
Recorded at live concerts in Montreal and Europe; No Man's Land, Hemel Hempstead; East West, Los Angeles; Spin Studios, New York; Outhouse studio; and studio sessions for The Raven That Refused To Sing and Hand. Cannot. Erase.
Release date: January 2016
Highest chart placings: UK: 21, US: 114
Running time: 36:14
Record label: Kscope

Steven Wilson released the *4½* mini-album in 2016, an interim release between his fourth studio album *Hand. Cannot. Erase.* and his fifth *To The Bone*. All tracks were written and recorded during the *Hand. Cannot. Erase.* sessions, except 'Year Of The Plague', which was recorded during the sessions for *The Raven That Refused To Sing*, and 'Don't Hate Me', a Porcupine Tree song that was recorded on the 2015 European tour. Wilson told Greg Prato of *Songfacts* in February 2016 that although the record isn't a concept album, it's still carefully sequenced.

'My Book Of Regrets' (9:23)

Hand. Cannot. Erase. was originally called 'My Book Of Regrets' and was based on a different concept. Two of the 'regret' songs, 'First Regret' and 'Regret #9', appear on the main album.

The entry in the *Hand. Cannot. Erase.* blog dated 12 December 2014 is called 'My Book Of Regrets', and the 20 May 2010 entry includes a line that is very similar to the opening of the song: 'Gazing out through a taxi window at the streets of London on a Saturday night is like watching reality TV with the sound turned down'. The blog marks one of the few times that the protagonist is seen socialising, going to a leaving do for a work colleague, before she returns in the taxi to her 'solipsistic cocoon'. The song is seen mostly from the protagonist's point of view, recording her slightly lurid fascination with London's nightlife, including a reference to kids in shopping malls that touches on the theme of disaffected youth that was so important on Porcupine Tree's 2007 album *Fear Of A Blank Planet*. The protagonist says, 'all of this can be read/In my book of regrets' – presumably a reference to her blog.

The song starts with Pete Townshend-style guitar chords, reminiscent of the Porcupine Tree classic 'Arriving Somewhere But Not Here' (*Deadwing*, 2005).

At around 2:30, the guitar becomes more agitated, changing frenetically from minor to major and back. There's a lovely, free-flowing bassline, a Moog keyboard solo and a blistering guitar solo from Dave Kilminster. The riffs become more proggy as the band take flight. At around 5:15, the song dissolves into a very *Hand. Cannot. Erase.* spacey section, and Wilson adds another guitar solo, initially laid-back, then more searching and bluesy. The voice returns with Wilson singing very sweetly. The track ends with a short coda, reprising the opening section with added harmony vocals, followed by a gentle sigh.

'Year Of The Plague' (4:15)
This instrumental track was recorded during the sessions for *The Raven,* but it's simple rather than virtuosic, unlike many of the tracks on that album. It's gentle and thoughtful, haunting even. It begins with echoey Fender Rhodes chords and mysterious synthesised strings, then guitar arpeggios play alternating chords, while a lovely synth melody floats above. The instrumentation becomes richer as the song progresses, but it never strays from the original idea. It's a moment of beauty, frozen in time.

'Happiness III' (4:31)
Released as a single in October 2016
One of many bitter songs about relationships in Wilson's catalogue. The title is brutally ironic. The protagonist is bored and frustrated, but there's also a much darker side: 'Sorry if I'm rude/I'm getting anxious and a darker mood comes over me'. He pushes his partner over on the ice, apparently so he can catch her when she falls, but actually to cause her injury. There's another reference to the shopping mall from *Fear Of A Blank Planet* and to being bored by online pornography, perhaps suggesting that the two protagonists are the same person.

There's also a trace of the more personal theme of creativity and whether life has any significance, which has often troubled Wilson, dating back to the early days of Porcupine Tree and the 'stupid dream' of being a rock star expressed in the 1999 album of the same name. Not getting out of bed because there's nothing new to say was also referred to by the piano teacher in the song 'Piano Lessons': 'You'd better give up hoping/You're better off in bed'.

The song is fairly straightforward and rocky in style, with brutal, spiky guitar, robust bass and rock 'n' roll keyboards. The vocal delivery is raw at times, which suits the song's sentiments.

'Sunday Rain Sets In' (3:50)
Another instrumental, spacey and atmospheric with a hint of mystery. Wilson plays guitar in the languid style of his friend and collaborator Mikael Åkerfeldt. At around 3:00, the track tries briefly to rouse itself from the torpor

of a rainy Sunday afternoon, but without success. One of many examples of music that Wilson has written that would be perfect for a movie soundtrack, although to date, he hasn't written any, despite various attempts to have the *Deadwing* project filmed.

'Vermillioncore' (5:09)

This instrumental is an exuberant exercise in repeating the same jazzy, syncopated riff in fascinating variations, with free jazz basslines and avant-garde angular keyboards. It's a joy to listen to, one of the highlights of the album. It's clearly a favourite of Wilson's – he played it 140 times on the 2018/19 *To The Bone* world tour.

'Don't Hate Me' (9:34)

Written in 1998 and originally released by Porcupine Tree on *Stupid Dream* (1999). This version was taken from a live concert in Europe in September 2015, with additional recording at No Man's Land.

A song about unrequited love, it begins with an image of a deserted London as light snow falls. For once, the image of a train doesn't represent Wilson's nostalgia for his childhood but the emptiness of the scene, as no-one gets on or off. A relationship has broken up, and weary resignation haunts the verses of the song. The chorus is more impassioned, as the unrequited lover, who is tired and lonely, makes a plea not to be hated, moderated by the deeply sarcastic line, 'I'm not special like you'.

Wilson duets with the Israeli singer Ninet Tayeb, who also featured memorably on 'Routine' on *Hand. Cannot. Erase.* The duet makes the contrast between the verse and the chorus even clearer. Tayeb's rich mezzo soprano is an inspired choice – she sings in the same octave as Wilson does on the Porcupine Tree version, as low in her range as he is high in his, making her intense vocals in the chorus sultrier but equally passionate.

It's fascinating to compare the playing on the two versions. The Porcupine Tree version features Chris Maitland on drums, Richard Barbieri on keyboards and Colin Edwin on bass. On *4½,* Craig Blundell is on drums, Adam Holzman on keyboards and Nick Beggs on bass. Theo Travis plays flute on the Porcupine Tree version and saxophone on both versions.

In the jazzy interlude, the later version features the quicksilver keyboards of Holzman, compared with Travis's mournful, lonely flute in the original. In some ways, the contrast between the bass players is the most interesting. Edwin's playing is loose, syncopated, with a warm tone. Nick Beggs' playing is more focused in tone, angular, tightly rhythmic and funky.

Bonus Tracks

In August 2017, Wilson told Paul Sinclair of *Super Deluxe Edition* he felt conflicted about releasing bonus tracks. He accepted that by releasing them on deluxe editions of the albums, he was depriving fans of some of the 'mystery'. But if he released an album without bonus tracks, then fans would be able to stream the full album, so 'many people would feel they didn't need to buy the physical product at all.' Many of the bonus tracks are demo versions of songs that are discussed in detail in the main chapters. Tracks that don't appear elsewhere are discussed below.

Insurgentes

'Port Rubicon' (4:24)

Possibly the darkest, most avant-garde track Wilson has ever written, channelling the terrible beauty of Scott Walker's 2006 album *The Drift*, and the noise rock of some of the tracks on *Insurgentes* itself. It begins with an uneasy soundscape and spoken words from Susana Moyaho, suddenly obliterated by a chunk of visceral noise with menacing drums. A muted section follows, with a distant saxophone from Theo Travis and atonal vocal melodies from Wilson that are as quietly horrifying as the noise that comes before. A human being (or a creature?) can be heard breathing ominously in the background. The wall of noise returns and the track ends with out-of-tune guitars. A deliciously unsettling track.

'Puncture Wound' (4:18)

This sounds remarkably like *A Forest* by The Cure, which Wilson covered on *Cover Version*. Both tracks begin with a distinctive four-note sequence starting with a minor third. The rhythm of the words in the verses is very similar, and the heavily chorused bass guitar is reminiscent of the sound of Simon Gallup. The sour-sounding synth is, however, very characteristic of *Insurgentes* and the chorus has an epic feel which is unique to the song, as are the surreal lyrics, such as 'Streets, like Prussian blues/Split the cells in my blood'. Despite being rather derivative, it has a certain dark majesty.

'Collecting Space' (5:10)

A lovely instrumental, featuring koto playing from Michiyo Yagi, who also plays on the title track of *Insurgentes*, and lively bass playing from Tony Levin. The melody at about 1:00 is a pre-echo of the opening of the verse melody of 'Dignity' on Porcupine Tree's 2022 album *Closure/Continuation*. The guitar solos, probably played on a PRS (Paul Reed Smith) guitar, have a warm, honeyed sound.

'Insurgentes (Mexico)' (5:45)

The original version of the title track, unusual in being written and recorded live, during the night of 28 February 2008 in Ex Templo de Santa Teresa La Antigua, Mexico City.

'The 78' (4:47)

This track was originally released as a 'hidden' untitled track at the end of the second disc of the *Insurgentes* deluxe box set. It then became the B-side to the 'Harmony Korine' 7" single, when it was given the name 'The 78'. The song starts with ominous low synth drones, fierce drumming, and sharp guitar stabs with short slapback echo. It soon turns into an indie rock epic on the subject of throwing one's life away.

'A Western Home' (3:09)

On the *Insurgentes* DVD, Wilson said he originally planned to create his first solo album by completing various songs that didn't fit on other albums. Instead, in a burst of creativity, he started writing new songs in 'quite a different style.' This left only one of the previous tracks, 'A Western Home', that he completed in the sessions for the new album. Written in 2001, it inevitably has a Porcupine Tree feel. After the opening piano chords, the prog metal guitar riff and rhythmic spoken words are similar to the title track of *Deadwing* (2005). The words 'Kneel and disconnecting' relate to the title of the song 'Kneel And Disconnect' (*The Incident,* 2009). Other lyrics, such as 'with no heart I can kill you', seem to relate to the dark theme of inhuman serial killers on several of the tracks on *In Absentia* (2002), particularly 'Strip The Soul'.

'Deadwing Theme' (1:47)

This instrumental track, originally released only on Myspace, dates back to 2004 when Wilson and director Mike Bennion were working on the *Deadwing* film project for which they had written a script and Wilson had written some music. The project didn't get off the ground, but some of the music was used on the Porcupine Tree album of the same name. It features a disturbing, chromatic piano theme and a lovely chord sequence, with the same creepy breathing as on 'Port Rubicon' (see above).

'Desperation' (6:16)

On the *Insurgentes* DVD, Wilson said he recorded about 30 tracks for the album, ten of which were included on the final release. This track wasn't finished and mixed until January 2010. It starts with the same sour-sounding synth sound as 'Desperation' and 'Puncture Wound', then a bass riff that would probably have been played in a prog-metal distorted style if it had been on a late Porcupine Tree album, but here it is played in a cleaner style. The chorused lead guitar is very much in the style of Robert Smith of The Cure. The vocals are distorted in the style of Nine Inch Nails. Gavin Harrison provides robust drums.

'Insurgentes' (Sweet Billy Pilgrim Mix) (5:20)

A remix of the title track by English band Sweet Billy Pilgrim.

Grace For Drowning

'Home In Negative' (3:00)

This song appears to be about being trapped in a relationship, the title suggesting an image of the home in which the colours are reversed as in a photographic negative, but there's also a metaphorical view of the home seen by an outsider in a negative way. The protagonist seems to be trapped for 'a hundred years' in the woods outside the house, under a spell from a witch. It's an image from a fairy tale, but also a metaphor for the unequal nature of the relationship: 'You're antisocial but you make my day/I'll always stay with you come what may'. Although the subject matter is depressing, the song is wistful, pared back in its subtle melancholy. The track suddenly springs into bloom at 1:58 on the words 'So I wait through the winter', with a lovely Beatles-like melody.

'Fluid Tap' (5:45)

A fluid tap is a medical procedure for draining fluid from the abdomen. Although the lyrics are fairly obscure, it appears that there is a killer at work here, violating a doctor's basic duty to 'first do no harm'. It seems we are back in the world of serial killers explored in Porcupine Tree's *In Absentia* (2002). The lyrics hint at dark, murderous crimes without being explicit. The song benefits from a superb King Crimson rhythm section, with Pat Mastelotto on drums and Tony Levin on Chapman Stick providing a pulsating contrast to the slow-moving malevolence of the keyboards and vocals.

'The Map' (3:30)

As mentioned in the *Grace For Drowning* chapter, one of the album's themes is Wilson's struggle to be a successful musician, a theme he visited on the Porcupine Tree album *Stupid Dream* in 1999. So, the title of this instrumental could refer to that dilemma, and the upbeat electronic percussion contrasted with the slow synth chords suggests the ambivalent feelings Wilson has had about his career over the years. This may be a fanciful interpretation, but it remains a very strong track that would work as the theme tune for a film or TV series.

'Raider Acceleration' (6:15)

A jazz-rock instrumental featuring Wilson on bass, Nic France on drums, Theo Travis on sax and Mike Outram on guitar. The title refers to 'Raider II' on the main album, which also features long, improvised passages. The track's status as a demo is revealed by the hiss at the start and the metronome count-in. The bass guitar riff is repeated throughout almost the whole song, as the virtuoso guest players work their magic. The repeated musical motif is a complex polyrhythmic sequence, mostly in 6/8 but with extra beats at times, giving the track a very prog/jazz feel. It seems strongly influenced by King Crimson, hardly surprising, bearing in mind Wilson's use of musicians from the band on several of his tracks and his extensive remixing work for the band.

'Black Dog Throwbacks' (2:30)

An ambient instrumental made up from vocal samples, similar in texture and feel to 'Light Mass Prayers', from the 1996 Porcupine Tree album *Signify*, written by the band's drummer Chris Maitland. The reference to 'throwbacks' in the title suggests that the track refers back to 'Remainder The Black Dog'.

'Cut Ribbon' (6.58)

Wilson released this song on Soundcloud in December 2011. He said it was written in 2001 for a possible 'metal style collaboration' with Mikael Åkerfeldt, and it has strong heavy metal riffs, making it an 'orphan song' for which Wilson never found a home – his eventual collaboration with Åkerfeldt under the Storm Corrosion name was more like psychedelic folk than heavy metal. He originally uploaded a version to his iPhone app, then recorded a new version with Gavin Harrison on drums during the *Grace For Drowning* sessions in 2008. The lyrics are very sparse, and the meaning feels just out of reach. They do include the words 'Collapse the light into the earth', the title of a song on Porcupine Tree's *In Absentia* (2002). It's a superb track, with thrilling riffs, strong melodies, dynamic contrasts and a mesmerising outro that's reminiscent of Opeth at their best.

The Raven That Refused To Sing

'Clock Song' (4:31)

A very simple instrumental ballad, mostly played on solo piano. Some commentators on YouTube have commented that it would have made a very good intro or outro to the album, but it feels too underdeveloped to earn its place with the prog epics there. It's still quietly haunting, though. Carol Hartung, commenting on YouTube, summed up its effect nicely, 'like stars twinkling around the moon...'

Hand. Cannot. Erase.

'Key Of Skeleton' (Demo) (4:06)

This instrumental track begins with keyboards and strings similar to those at the start of *I Am The Walrus* from The Beatles' 1967 double EP *Magical Mystery Tour*. Muscular drums soon join in, with a pleasantly 1960s feel to the guitar. The song has that feeling of inevitability that some of the best instrumental tracks have, until it's nicely subverted towards the end as it takes a dark turn.

'Piano Themes From Hand Cannot Erase' (2:20)

A short suite of themes from the album played on solo piano in a slightly jazzy style.

'Last Regret' (Demo) (3:08)
This is an early version of 'Happy Returns', a song addressed to the female protagonist's brother on the main album, but with a different set of lyrics. It shares that song's ambiguity – the final phrase is 'The traffic sings me back to sleep/And the world just slips away...' This could simply refer to her drifting off to sleep, or to her leaving the world either in death or at the hands of aliens (see the main chapter for a discussion about what may happen to the protagonist). The song ends with the 'doo, doo, doo' vocal section from 'Happy Returns'.

To The Bone
'Ask Me Nicely (Intro)' (1:42)
'Ask Me Nicely' (3:53)
Wilson told Anil Prasad of *Innerviews* in 2017 that at one point, he was planning to call *To The Bone* by the title of this song instead. The common phrase 'If you can't be polite/Say nothing at all' is used throughout the track, reflecting the idea that 'people can be so rude, short-tempered and aggressive', according to Wilson. Instead, he used the title for the 'making of' video documentary directed by Lasse Hoile that came with the Deluxe Edition and DVD-audio version of the album.

The short 'Intro' features birdsong, the opening ambient chords and the first section of the main song. The full version of the song replaces the birdsong with spoken words, which are not quite decipherable in the mix. There are some lovely backing vocals, which have a haunting quality, but the song feels unfinished. From around 2:30, there's a livelier instrumental section with robust drumming.

'A Door Marked Summer' (7:41)
In 2017, YouTube commentator Lily O'Chops perfectly summed up this song, describing it as a 'long, languid, golden, ethereal afternoon.' Several others rightly commented that it should have been on the main album. It feels like a Porcupine Tree song, not least because it starts with the same acoustic guitar chords as 'Drown With Me' from *In Absentia* (2002). But the comparison goes deeper as the song is made up of a series of separate episodes like a classic Porcupine Tree song, disparate elements that are beautifully crafted together to create a coherent whole. Interestingly, in his book *Limited Edition Of One,* Steven Wilson refers to a track by art-rock band 10cc (from Stockport, England) called 'I'm Mandy Fly Me' from their 1976 album *How Dare You!* (a shortened version was released as a single). Wilson calls the song a 'slice of brilliance', equal to The Beach Boys' classic *Good Vibrations* (1966). He praises the song for moving through various 'scenes' like watching a movie. Wilson has often said that he views his own songs as movies in their structure, and it's fascinating that Wilson's songwriting style could have been influenced as much by 10cc as by the long-form epics of prog rock.

'Northern Cyclonic' (3:50)
A beautiful ambient instrumental track with heavy percussion, possibly influenced by Boards of Canada or by Peter Gabriel's 1986 album *So*. It's notable for the amount of harmonic invention, whereas many of the most successful ambient tracks deliberately remain in the same key to create a transcendent atmosphere rather than melodic interest. Like the other bonus tracks listed above, it probably didn't make the final album simply because it didn't fit the more hard-edged feel, rather than because of any lack of quality.

'Antisocial' (7" Single) (3:11)
Only available with the Deluxe Edition as a one-sided 7" single in its own picture sleeve. According to the journal in the Deluxe Edition, it was originally meant to be the introduction to 'The People Who Eat Darkness'. It works well as a standalone instrumental, as the album track would have felt too long at over nine minutes. The main thing it adds to the album track is some interesting harmonic progressions, particularly at 1:23 when a rising chromatic figure sounds rather like the main riff from 'Shot By Both Sides', the 1978 single by Manchester post-punk band Magazine.

Singles

Insurgentes

'Harmony Korine'/'The 78' (February 2009)

Grace For Drowning

'Postcard' (October 2011):
'Postcard' (4.28)
'Postcard' (Live Piano/Vocal Version) (3.12)

'Postcard' (North Atlantic Oscillation Remix) (4.38) (October 2011)
Remixed by Scottish post-progressive rock and electronic band North Atlantic Oscillation, signed to Kscope Records, this is quite different from the original. It drenches the opening piano chords in echo, adding a heavy kick drum to signify that this will be an electronic/dance version, but retaining Wilson's intense, sweetly intimate vocals. The insistent piano motif is replaced by a keyboard riff that has the spikiness of a harpsichord. Dance percussion and airy synth chords are added, and the ethereal choir of the original is introduced much earlier than in the original. At 2.30, Wilson's voice is heavily compressed against a resolute bass drum, then the track bursts into glorious bloom before a gentle fade.

'Index' (Necro Deathmort Remix) (5.01) (October 2011)
Remixed by electronic duo Necro Deathmort, formed in London in 2007. This version removes the precise and incisive dissection of the protagonist's obsessive personality in the original and concentrates instead on the underlying horror of the protagonist's actions. In doing so, it also distances us from any sense of compassion we may have for the protagonist. The almost militaristic percussion of the original is replaced by a wash of distortion, and the chorus vocals are almost obliterated.

4½

'Happiness III'/'Space Oddity' (Live) (David Bowie) (October 2016)

To The Bone

'Pariah' (May 2017)
'The Same Asylum As Before', 'Song Of I', 'Permanating' (all June 2017)
'Refuge' (August 2017)

Other Singles

'Vapour Trail Lullaby' (9.18) (October 2010)
A single-track CD single given away free with pre-orders of the *Insurgentes* DVD. The song has a complicated history, as Wilson explained on his website. He wrote it for Porcupine Tree's seventh studio album *In Absentia* (2002), but when the album 'developed in a heavier direction', the band

dropped it. It then appeared on *Blackfield*, the first Blackfield album in 2004, in a stripped-down version called 'Lullaby'. Wilson revisited it when recording *Insurgentes,* but didn't feel it fitted the more experimental style of that album, although he did adapt the coda section into the short instrumental album track 'Twilight Coda'. In the end, he went back to the demo version: 'I find I still prefer the original demo version from 2001, so that is the one I have decided to include here.'

The lyrics share some of the dark brutality of the songs on *In Absentia*. The protagonist endures a damagingly dependent relationship, almost like the unlikely affection that can develop between a kidnapper and their victim (Stockholm Syndrome). The extremes of the relationship are described in the words, 'Never part/Break my heart'. The short, brutal lines of the verses contrast with the much longer repeated phrase that makes up the chorus, 'How does it feel without your drugs?' This is sung in an almost sarcastically innocent way, as if the protagonist has some power over the addressee, who is suffering withdrawal from drugs.

Although the song is reaching towards prog epic lengths for a single, the material is very simple. It retains interest by constantly shifting the musical arrangement. It begins with a circular piano motif and vocals apparently recorded on an answerphone in a 'note to self' mode. Guitar, drums, Hammond organ, full vocals and finally backing vocals are gradually added, like pieces of a jigsaw, until the whole picture becomes clear. The song drops away, then there's an ambient, wistful coda. A Mellotron drifts in as the song becomes psychedelic and spacey.

'Stoneage Dinosaurs' (Tim Smith) (4:15) (April 2011)

A split single with Manchester rock band Oceansize, covering the Cardiacs tracks 'Stoneage Dinosaurs' and 'Fear', Wilson contributing 'Stoneage Dinosaurs'. Released on white vinyl, this was limited to 2000 copies, with all profits going to Cardiacs' frontman Tim Smith following a heart attack in 2008. Smith died in July 2020, and Wilson wrote a tribute on YouTube on the day of his death: 'He had one of the few truly unique sounds and musical personalities you could ever hope to hear … a true original.' He described him as 'a cult artist, relatively under the radar for most of his career', which could serve as an apt description for Wilson himself.

'How Big The Space' (music by Steven Wilson; lyrics by Andy Partridge) (3.38) (April 2018)

Released for Record Store Day in April 2018. The B-side is a version of 'People Who Eat Darkness' from *To The Bone* called 'Ninet Version' (6.00), as it features Ninet Tayeb on vocals.

In 2017, Wilson told Anil Prasad of *Innerviews* that it didn't fit *To The Bone* because it's a '60s psychedelic-sounding song.' The lyrics by Andy Partridge, who also wrote the words for the title track of the album, are a beautifully poetic description of the end of a relationship, superbly contrasting the mundane – 'I think I'll change the locks' – with the existential:

How big the space inside an empty heart
How brave the face when orbits pull apart
How black the hole where universes fade
How vast the bed where both of us once laid

The best description of the song comes from Creighton Addison on YouTube in 2018: 'Please tell me I'm not the only one who thinks if [early] Pink Floyd had performed Radiohead's 'Karma Police', it would sound close to this...' The closing chord sounds very similar to the opening chord of Prince's 1984 single 'Let's Go Crazy'.

'Permanating' (Ewan Pearson Remix) (February 2018)
Ewan Pearson describes himself on his website as a 'Producer, Mixer and Remixer.' Pearson has had a lengthy career as a remixer, having worked with Tracey Thorn, Goldfrapp, Pet Shop Boys and Depeche Mode, among many others. To date, he has remixed three of Wilson's tracks: this one, 'Time Is Running Out' from *Harmonic Divergence* and the single 'Inclination', all in 2024. Pearson's remix of 'Permanating' is very similar to the original, making it even more upbeat. The fierce drums of the original are replaced by even heavier disco beats, the spoken word intro ('Somewhere on the highway...') is ditched and the guitar solo, which appears 90 seconds into the original, is left to the very end.

Films/Soundtracks

Insurgentes DVD (2010)

The *Insurgentes* film is a documentary on the making of the album of that name. The Kscope website described it as 'a musical road movie that follows the making of [the record] ... a portrait of an increasingly rare artist who works with music and media out of love and not for fame and fortune.'

Sometimes, the story is disrupted by avant-garde imagery, such as when a home studio session for 'Abandoner' is intercut with masked human beings crawling towards the camera. This anarchic imagery can provide a facetious commentary. For instance, as part of the travelogue, Wilson visits Disney World Resort in Florida and sarcastically sports Mickey Mouse ears. He listlessly embraces Minnie and has his photo taken with her and Mickey. He stands outside a sign for the Carousel of Progress animatronics show, carefully placed to cover the final letters so that it reads 'Carousel of Prog'. Elsewhere, Wilson talks about how heartbreaking it can be working in the contemporary music industry, and how criticism of his work can feel very personal. This intimate and rather bitter insight is punctuated by surreal images of people with birds' heads poking a severed hand with a stick.

The documentary was made by Lasse Hoile. Wilson and Hoile share a love of European art films. Some of the imagery could be from a film by the Spanish director Luis Buñuel, whose surrealism often takes everyday events and gives them a twist – like the dinner party that opens *The Exterminating Angel* (1962). Sometimes the imagery is more extreme, as in *Un Chien Andalou* (1929), which Buñuel made with the Spanish Surrealist artist Salvador Dalí. Hoile combines both elements, absurd creatures with studio and live footage, and Wilson interacting with fans and other musicians, to create a visually absorbing whole. Ironically, as Wilson said in the Twitter Listening Party for the *Insurgentes* album, hosted by Tim Burgess in June 2020: 'We ended up editing out a lot of the humour to make it more surreal and enigmatic, with the result that it added to my reputation for being humourless and miserable!' Sequences from Wilson's visit to Mexico to record parts of the album are also used very effectively, particularly his visit to the Island of the Dolls with its dismembered and cobwebbed dolls.

Equally fascinating is Wilson's return to his old school in Hemel Hempstead, England. He reminisces about his first ever live performance at the school disco in 1980: 'I was so nervous I couldn't stand up. I sat here at the side of the stage and played my guitar.' Thirteen years later, he made his live debut with Porcupine Tree, at the Nag's Head pub in High Wycombe, about 20 miles away. He suffered stage fright for many years: 'I used to spend the whole show staring at my shoes.' He's now very comfortable performing live, as can be seen on the *Home Invasion* DVD. On the *Insurgentes* DVD, he attributes his increasing confidence to the time he spent in Israel, helping him become more relaxed after he spent time with the people there, whom he regards as more friendly, less self-conscious and closed, and less stressed about life.

There are some charming exchanges with Wilson's parents. He fondly recalls how his father, an electronics engineer, built him some of the equipment that started him on his career as a recording musician. Sadly, his father died in 2011, not long after the discussion was filmed. Wilson is also seen talking to his mother about his teenage bands, Amber Dawn and Karma. When Wilson played in the back garden with one of his bands, the neighbours complained to his mother: 'We didn't think you would let that happen, Maureen.'

The documentary is also a commentary on the music industry. Wilson talks about growing up buying vinyl records with his pocket money, choosing carefully because he had to spend a lot of time, money and energy on each purchase. He compares that unfavourably with download culture, which allows you to obtain the whole of a band's back catalogue in minutes, and dismiss it just as easily and quickly. Fifteen years later, streaming has largely replaced downloading, but the basic point remains valid. He also criticises the use of low-quality MP3 files and the tiny image with each file compared with the artwork that comes with a vinyl LP. To express his frustration, Wilson can be seen destroying several iPods, with a gun, a blow torch, a hammer, a small blue car and a sledgehammer. As Wilson said on the Twitter Listening party, it was 'kinda silly, but it got me press.' For a while, fans used to bring their iPods to gigs for Wilson to smash.

The Last Day Of June (2017)

Steven Wilson's soundtrack to the adventure puzzle video game *Last Day Of June* is based on music from his solo albums, or as Bass Communion, from 2004-2016. Most of the music was specially remixed or edited for the soundtrack. It was released in a limited edition of 4,000 on 19 November 2021 and later on streaming services. The game was directed by Massimo Guarini, who was inspired by Wilson's song 'Drive Home' from *The Raven That Refused To Sing*, and the characters in Jess Cope's video. The Wilson tracks are: 'Some Things Cannot Be Changed' (2:58) ('Routine', *Hand. Cannot. Erase.*), 'That Day By The Pier' (3:58) ('Significant Other', *Insurgentes*), 'There Must Be A Way' (1:17) ('The Raven That Refused To Sing', *The Raven That Refused To Sing*), 'The Last Day Of June' (8:18) ('Belle De Jour', *Grace For Drowning*), 'Suspended In Me' (1:09) ('Year Of The Plague', *4½*), 'Driving Home' (1:39) ('Insurgentes', *Insurgentes*), 'I'm Still Here…' (1:35) ('Veneno Para Las Hadas', *Insurgentes*), 'Deceive' (1:07) ('Deform To Form A Star' *Grace For Drowning*), 'Together, Forever Again' (3:52) ('Track One', *Grace For Drowning*). The Bass Communion tracks are: 'The Boy Who Lost His Friends' (2:16) ('After Dark'), 'The Crib' (1:05) ('Haze 1402'), 'Time For A New Start' (3:27) ('Haze Shrapnel'), 'Suspended In You' (1:18) ('Ghost Part 5'), 'Under The Shadow Of My Father' (1:29) ('Loss Part 2A'), 'Accept' (4:13) ('Loss Part 2B').

Live Albums

Catalogue/Preserve/Amass (2012)

Personnel:
Steven Wilson: vocals, guitars, keyboards
Aziz Ibrahim: guitars
Nick Beggs: bass guitar, Chapman stick, backing vocals
Adam Holzman: keyboards, piano
Theo Travis: flute, saxophone
Marco Minnemann: drums
Recorded 'live in Europe' in October 2011
Release date: April 2012
Highest chart placings: did not chart
Running time: 70:11
Record label: Headphone Dust/Kscope
Current edition: not available

Steven Wilson's first live solo album was recorded on his first solo tour. Its title comes from the lyrics of 'Index', from *Grace For Drowning*. All tracks are from that album, except 'No Twilight Within The Courts Of The Sun' and 'Veneno Para Las Hadas' from *Insurgentes*. The vinyl edition, limited to 2000 copies, was released on Record Store Day on 21 April 2012. The CD version, limited to 3000 copies, was available to buy during the second leg of the 2012 tour in April and May.

Get All You Deserve (2012)

Personnel:
Steven Wilson: vocals, guitar, keyboards
Adam Holzman: keyboards
Marco Minnemann: drums
Nick Beggs: bass guitar, stick, backing vocals
Niko Tsonev: guitar
Theo Travis: saxophone, flute, clarinet, keyboards
Recorded at Teatro Metropólitan, Mexico City, on 13 April 2012
Release date: September 2012
Highest chart placings: did not chart
Running time: 2 hours 10 minutes
Record label: Kscope

Get All You Deserve was recorded at the Teatro Metropólitan, Mexico City, in April 2012 during the *Grace For Drowning* tour. It features tracks from Wilson's first two solo albums – *Insurgentes* ('No Twilight Within The Courts Of The Sun', 'Harmony Korine', 'Abandoner', 'Veneno Para Las Hadas', 'Get All You Deserve') and *Grace For Drowning* ('Index', 'Deform To Form A Star', 'Sectarian', 'Postcard', 'Remainder The Black Dog', 'Like Dust I Have Cleared From My Eye', 'No Part Of Me', 'Raider II'). There's also a preview of 'Luminol' from *The Raven That Refused To Sing*. The concert is bookended by tracks from another of Wilson's solo projects, Bass Communion. The video was filmed by Lasse Hoile.

Home Invasion: In Concert At The Royal Albert Hall (2018)
Personnel:
Steven Wilson: vocals, guitar, keyboards
Alex Hutchings: guitar
Adam Holzman: keyboards
Ninet Tayeb: vocals on 'Pariah', 'People Who Eat Darkness', 'Blank Tapes', 'Routine'
Nick Beggs: bass
Craig Blundell: drums
Recorded live on 29 March 2018
Release date: November 2018 (DVD/CD), March 2019 (five-LP vinyl box set)
Highest chart placing: did not chart
Running time: 2 hours 33 minutes
Record label: Eagle Vision/Caroline International
Home Invasion was recorded on the final night of Wilson's three-night residency at the Royal Albert Hall in London in March 2018. The concerts were part of the *To The Bone* world tour, which lasted over a year, with 145 shows performed to over 250,000 people in 33 countries. The album features the complete *To The Bone* album, except, rather strangely, the title track. It includes four tracks from *Hand. Cannot. Erase.* – 'Home Invasion/Regret #9', 'Ancestral', 'Routine' and 'Hand Cannot Erase' (the last two are rehearsal tracks on the Blu-Ray and vinyl editions only). 'Vermillioncore' is from the *4½* EP. Porcupine Tree's back catalogue is represented by 'The Creator Has A Mastertape', '[The] Sound Of Muzak' and 'Heartattack In A Layby' (Blu Ray and vinyl only, all from *In Absentia*); 'Sleep Together' (*Fear Of A Blank Planet*) 'Arriving Somewhere But Not Here', 'Lazarus' (*Deadwing*); 'Even Less' (*Stupid Dream*). The vinyl set also includes 'How Is Your Life Today?' from *Lightbulb Sun* by Porcupine Tree, 'Blackfield' from the first Blackfield album, and 'Postcard' from *Grace For Drowning*. The concert ends with the title track from *The Raven That Refused To Sing*. All tracks were written by Wilson except 'Blackfield', which is co-written with Aviv Geffen. The Porcupine Tree tracks are analysed in detail in the book *Porcupine Tree On Track* by Nick Holmes (Sonicbond Publishing, 2021; revised and updated March 2025).

Bibliography And References

General

Stevenwilsonhq.com
Archive.org
Discogs.com
Kscopemusic.com
SongMeanings.com
starsdie.com (archived)
Reddit.com
YouTube
Soundcloud.com
X/Twitter
Discogs.com
Tim Burgess' Twitter Listening Party @LISTENING_PARTY
Häberle, U., *Steven Wilson The Complete Discography* (11th Edition, August 2021)
Wilson, S., Wall, M., *Limited Edition Of One – How To Succeed In The Music Industry Without Being Part Of The Mainstream*, Special Edition in two volumes with CD (Constable, an imprint of Little, Brown, April 2022)

Insurgentes

Bennett, S., 'Keeping Busy with Steven Wilson', *Tape Op Magazine* (Sept/Oct 2009 edition)
Brown, H., 'Mike Oldfield interview: 'I am a man of extremes'', *The Telegraph* (March 2014)
Bunney, D., 'Steven Wilson Interview on his Debut Solo Album *Insurgentes*', Edge Radio Tasmania (March 2009)
Castiglioni, B., 'Gavin Harrison Forum', *Drummerworld* (May 2011)
Deadwing, 'Porcupine Tree's Steven Wilson Discusses His Heavier Side', *Metal Underground* (March 2009)
Humphries, S., 'An Eclectic Master Craftsman: An Interview With Steven Wilson', *PopMatters* (March 2009)
Jeff (no last name given), 'Steven Wilson interview', *MetalStorm* (April 2009)
Jenks, F., 'Steven Wilson/Porcupine Tree ... with Frank Jenks', *Listen In FULL* (August 2010)
McClelland, R., 'Steven Wilson Interview EXCLUSIVE', *guitarguitar.co.uk* (April 2021)
'Steven Wilson Interview', *Recording Magazin* (January 2014)
'Wilson, Steven – *Insurgentes* (Limited Edition) – Round Table Review', *Dutch Progressive Rock Page* (December 2008)

Grace For Drowning

gracefordrowning.com (archived)
'Ten Life Sentences for BTK Killer', BBC News Website (August 2005)
bencastle.com

Davey, M., Hart, A., McElroy, M., 'Suspect in 10 Kansas Murders Lived an Intensely Ordinary Life', *New York Times* (March 2005)
Fowles, J., *The Collector* (Jonathan Cape, 1963; Vintage Classics, 2004)
Gillespie, J., Brooks, R. 'The serial killer next door gave rise to BBC hit', *The Sunday Times* (June 2013)
Hoile, L., *The Making Of In Absentia* (documentary film from *In Absentia* deluxe edition 2020)
Humphries, S., 'Grace Under Pressure: An Interview With Steven Wilson', *PopMatters* (August 2011)
Koch, K., 'What Near-Death Experiences Reveal about the Brain', *Scientific American* (June 2020)
Moon, G., 'Steven Wilson on *Grace For Drowning*', *Prog* (2011; republished September 2019)
Ott, T., 'BTK Killer: A Timeline of His Murders, Reappearance and Capture', *Biograpy.com* (August 2021)
Prasad, A., 'Steven Wilson Art as a Mirror', *Innerviews* (2012)
Reid, G., 'Steve [sic] Wilson Of Porcupine Tree Interviewed (2011): Setting Controls To The Heart Of His Prog', *Elsewhere Magazine* (September 2011)
Rosen, S., 'Steven Wilson: 'Porcupine Tree Was Gonna Be A One-Off Thing'', *Ultimate-Guitar.com* (December 2011)
Skarin, R., 'Steven Wilson 2012 Community Q&A – Steven Answers Your Questions!', *starsdie.com* (July 2012)
Simkiss A. J., 'Obligated To Collect: A Visual Analysis Of Steven Wilson's 'Index'', *theodysseyonline.com* (November 2015)
Thodoris, 'Interview: Steven Wilson (solo, Porcupine Tree, Blackfield, No-Man)', Hit Channel (Greece) (April 2012)
Trenwith, R., 'Steven Wilson – *Grace For Drowning*', *DPRP* (September 2011)

The Raven That Refused To Sing (And Other Stories)

Bosso, J., 'Steven Wilson talks *The Raven That Refused To Sing (And Other Stories)*', *Music Radar* (February 2013)
Burns, L., 'Interpreting Transmedia and Multimodal Narratives – Steven Wilson's *The Raven That Refused To Sing*', *The Routledge Companion To Popular Music Analysis: Expanding Approaches* (2020)
Cope, J., 'Steven Wilson – The Making of 'Drive Home'', YouTube (October 2013)
Davenport, T., 'Steven Wilson: 'My Biggest Ambition Is To Score A Movie' and 'Records Sounded Best In The 70s'', *Ultimate-Guitar.com* (February 2013)
Ewing, J., 'The story of Steven Wilson's *Hand. Cannot. Erase.*', *Prog* (February 2015)
Metal Blast, 'Kill your iPod: An Interview with Steven Wilson', YouTube (November 2013)
Miers, J., 'A Conversation with Steven Wilson of Porcupine Tree', *The Buffalo News* (April 2013)

Prasad, A., 'Steven Wilson: Past Presence', *Innerviews* (2013)
Ravenscroft, K., 'The Holy DRINKER', PassionArt (undated)
Rotondi, J., 'Interview: Steven Wilson – Of Ravens, Revenants, and Creeping Things', *Premier Guitar* (April 2013)
Trenwith, R., Francis, B., Palladino, G. and Henderson, A., 'Steven Wilson – *The Raven That Refused To Sing (And Other Stories)* – Round Table Review', *DPRP* (March 2013)
Wakim, S., 'Interview: Hajo Müller', *Street Art United States* (March 2016)

Hand. Cannot. Erase.

handcannoterase.com (archived)
@handcannoterase on Twitter (posted from January to March 2015 only)
César, 'Hand Cannot Erase hidden riddle', *Quadraphonicquad* (May 2018)
'EastWest Steven Wilson's Ghostwriter', *Sweetwater.com* (undated, accessed August 2022)
Eastwest website *(soundsonline.com)*
Ewing, J., 'The story of Steven Wilson's *Hand. Cannot. Erase.*', *Prog* (February 2015)
Gabryel, S., 'Thanks to Karolina, Steven Wilson shows Pozna' to the world', *Głos Wielkopolski* (April 2016)
Humphries, S., 'Steven Wilson Hiding in Plain Sight', *Under The Radar* (March 2015)
Mettler, M., 'Pushing the aural envelope with high-res audio evangelist Steven Wilson', *Digital Trends* (March 2015)
Morley, C., 'Joyce Carol Vincent: How could this young woman lie dead and undiscovered for almost three years?', *The Observer* (October 2011)
Pautasso, L., '[Interview] STEVEN WILSON', *Reverb Online* (August 2016)
Pedrotti, F., 'Steven Wilson: 'Every Time I Go On Stage I Can Get Shot', *FabrizioPedrotti.com* (May 2018)
Prato, G., 'Steven Wilson of Porcupine Tree', *Songfacts* (February 2016)
Simon, P., '*Hand. Cannot. Erase.* – An Interview With Steven Wilson', *HuffPost* (January 2015)
Rallo, A-C., 'The Routine of Denial. Steven Wilson's Routine: A Sartrean Journey Into Existentialism' (*Collecting Space. Essays On The Work Of Steven Wilson*, Anesthetize Productions, 2017)
Simpson, D., 'Steven Wilson: the prog rocker topping the charts without anyone noticing', *The Guardian* (August 2017)
Starkey, J., 'Woman Dead in Flat for 3 Years', *The Sun* (April 2006)
Witte, K., and others, 'Steven Wilson – *Hand. Cannot. Erase.* – Round Table Review', *DPRP* (February 2015)
YouTube, 'Steven Wilson Interview (Part 1)', *Face Culture* (January 2015)
Zivitz, J., 'Jazz fest: Steven Wilson – the complete conversation', *Montreal Gazette* (June 2015)

To The Bone

'Eight of Steven Wilson's Favourite Albums', *Uncut* (September 2017)
'Orlando nightclub shooting: How the attack unfolded', BBC News website (15 June 2016)
'Why is there a crisis in Calais?', BBC News website (3 October 2015)
Bellini, J., 'Steven Wilson: I've sacrificed family for music', YouTube (January 2017)
Bland, B., 'Steven Wilson *To The Bone*', *Drowned In Sound* (August 2017)
Ezell, B., 'A Specialist In Dying Arts: An Interview With Steven Wilson', *PopMatters* (August 2017)
Grady, K., 'Interview: Steven Wilson, progressive rock's biggest star talks about truth, touring and *To The Bone*', *Upside Adelaide* (September 2018)
Graham, A. L., 'Steven Wilson – Cutting It To The Bone', *Classic Rock Revisited* (undated)
Hann, M., 'The changing man: Has Steven Wilson ditched prog for pop?', *Prog* (August 2017)
Hoile, L., 'Ask Me Nicely (The Making of *To The Bone*)', Documentary published in Deluxe Edition and DVD-A (Blu-ray) edition of the album (August 2017)
Humphries, S., '*To The Bone*, A Track-By-Track Guide', *Steven Wilson HQ* (August 2017)
Mettler, M., 'On *To The Bone*, Steven Wilson crafts accessible songs that transcend time', *Digital Trends* (August 2017
McAfee, P., 'Steven Wilson – *To The Bone* – Round Table Review', *DPRP* (August 2017)
Morgan, C., 'Steven Wilson reveals the stories behind his album *To The Bone* – track by track and interview', *The Telegraph* (August 2017)
'Oxford Languages Word of the Year 2016', *Oxford University Press* (November 2016)
Perry, S. K., 'How a Rapist/Murderer Nearly Got Away With It [Book review of *People Who Eat Darkness* by Richard Lloyd Parry]', *Psychology Today* (June 2012)
Pedrotti, F., – see above
Prasad, A., 'Perceptions of Reality', *Innerviews* (2017)
Prato, G., 'Steven Wilson of Porcupine Tree', *Songfacts* (February 2016)
Pritchett, C., 'Interview with Steven Wilson – *To The Bone*', *World Prog-Nation* (August 2017)
Sinclair, P., 'Steven Wilson interview: *To The Bone*', *Super Deluxe Edition* (August 2017)
Wilding, P., 'Steven Wilson – *To The Bone* album review: Steven Wilson stays resolutely one step ahead', *Prog* (August 2017)
Wilson, S., '*To The Bone* transcribed for Piano – Vocal – Guitar TAB', *Hal Leonard* (September 2018)

Compilations, EPs, Bonus Tracks And Singles

Adrianbenavides.com
beatlesstory.com/blog/song-facts-sgt-pepper
ewanpearson.com
Kscopemusic.com/stevenwilson/insurgentes/remix-competition (archived)
Patmastelotto.com/steven-wilson-remixes
Chinen, N., 'Territory of Two Norwegian Trumpeters', *New York Times* (June 2009)
Cox, T., 'Interview with Bill Bruford from Auditory Illusions', BBC Radio 4 documentary (2 September 2019)
Grady, K., 'Interview: Steven Wilson, Progressive Rock's Biggest Star Talks About Truth, Touring And *To The Bone*', *Upside Adelaide* (September 2018)
History of the BBC/Anniversaries BBC Radiophonic Workshop founded 1 April 1958 (bbc.com)
Kielty, M., 'Lonely Robot release 'In Floral Green' video', *Prog* (August 2017)
May, T., 'I made mistakes but one year on I'm going Green for Grenfell', *Evening Standard* (June 2018)
Moon, G., 'Lonely Robot', *Prog* (June 2017)
Prasad, A., 'Perceptions of Reality', *Innerviews* (2017)
Prato, G., 'Steven Wilson of Porcupine Tree', *Songfacts* (February 2016)
Simpson, D., 'Steven Wilson: the prog rocker topping the charts without anyone noticing', *The Guardian* (August 2017)
Sinclair, P., 'Steven Wilson interview: *To The Bone*', *Super Deluxe Edition* (August 2017)
Wilson, S., 'Notes for the LP version of *Tape Experiments 1985/1986*', Tonefloat (2010)
Wilson, S., 'Notes for the CD version of *Unreleased Electronic Music'*, Headphone Dust (2017)

Porcupine Tree *Revised and Updated*

Every album, every song

Nick Holmes
Paperback
176 pages
41 colour photographs
978-1-78951-346-1
£16.99
$22.95

Every album and every song by these UK prog legends, fronted by Steven Wilson.

Porcupine Tree began in 1987 as a solo project for Steven Wilson but became a four-piece band when he was joined by Richard Barbieri, Colin Edwin, and Chris Maitland (later replaced by Gavin Harrison). Their first gig was in a pub in High Wycombe, England, in 1993, but by 2010, the band had toured Europe and America extensively, ending up playing to thousands of fans at a sold-out Royal Albert Hall in London. After a 12-year hiatus, the band returned in 2022 with a new album, *Closure/ Continuation* and extensive tours of arenas and festivals.

Although often labelled a progressive rock band, Porcupine Tree constantly changed style. Beginning by playing psychedelic music, Porcupine Tree experimented with space rock, dance, trance, melodic pop and electronica as well as prog rock. During a run of four albums from *In Absentia* in 2002, the band created a new hybrid of progressive metal riffs, melodic strength and rich vocal harmonies, with strong lyrics and powerful concepts. This aspect of the band has provided their most enduring legacy.

This revised and updated second edition, which includes a new chapter on *Closure/Continuation*, analyses in forensic detail all eleven of Porcupine Tree's studio albums, plus bonus tracks and Eps, providing illuminating insight into the band's music.

Would you like to write for Sonicbond Publishing?

At Sonicbond Publishing we are always on the look-out for authors, particularly for our two main series:

On Track. Mixing fact with in depth analysis, the On Track series examines the work of a particular musical artist or group. All genres are considered from easy listening and jazz to 60s soul to 90s pop, via rock and metal.

On Screen. This series looks at the world of film and television. Subjects considered include directors, actors and writers, as well as entire television and film series. As with the On Track series, we balance fact with analysis.

While professional writing experience would, of course, be an advantage the most important qualification is to have real enthusiasm and knowledge of your subject. First-time authors are welcomed, but the ability to write well in English is essential.

Sonicbond Publishing has distribution throughout Europe and North America, and all books are also published in E-book form. Authors will be paid a royalty based on sales of their book.

Further details are available from www.sonicbondpublishing.co.uk. To contact us, complete the contact form there or email info@sonicbondpublishing.co.uk